Year 5
Workbook

Pearson

Published by Pearson Education Limited, 80 Strand, London, WC2R 0RL.
www.pearson.com/international-schools

Copies of official specifications for all Pearson Edexcel qualifications may be found on the website:
https://qualifications.pearson.com

Text © Pearson Education Limited 2023
Produced by Just Content Ltd
Designed by PDQ Media Digital Media Solutions
Typeset by PDQ Media Digital Media Solutions
Picture research by Straive Ltd
Original illustrations © Pearson Education Limited 2023
Cover design © Pearson Education Limited 2023

The right of Lesley Butcher to be identified as the author of this work has been asserted by her in accordance with the
Copyright, Designs and Patents Act 1988.

First published 2023

26
10

British Library Cataloguing in Publication Data
A catalogue record for this book is available from the British Library

ISBN 978 1 292 43339 4

Printed in Italy by L.E.G.O. S.p.A.

Contents

1   Plant adaptations 2

2   Living things in danger 24

3   Diet and digestion.............................50

4   Mixing and separating materials 80

5   Earth and space 104

6   Seeing and reflecting 130

Plant adaptations

Plants are living things. They need light to make their food and the right temperature to grow well. Plants also need air and water. Adaptations help plants to survive in their habitat.

In this topic we will learn:

- that different habitats and microhabitats have different environmental conditions

- that plant roots take in water and that the availability of water may affect root growth

- that both plants and animals need oxygen from the air for respiration

- that plants need light and that the availability of light affects where they can grow

- to describe how plants are adapted to the environment they live in

- to compare plant adaptations in two contrasting habitats

- to predict the habitat of a plant by looking at its adaptations.

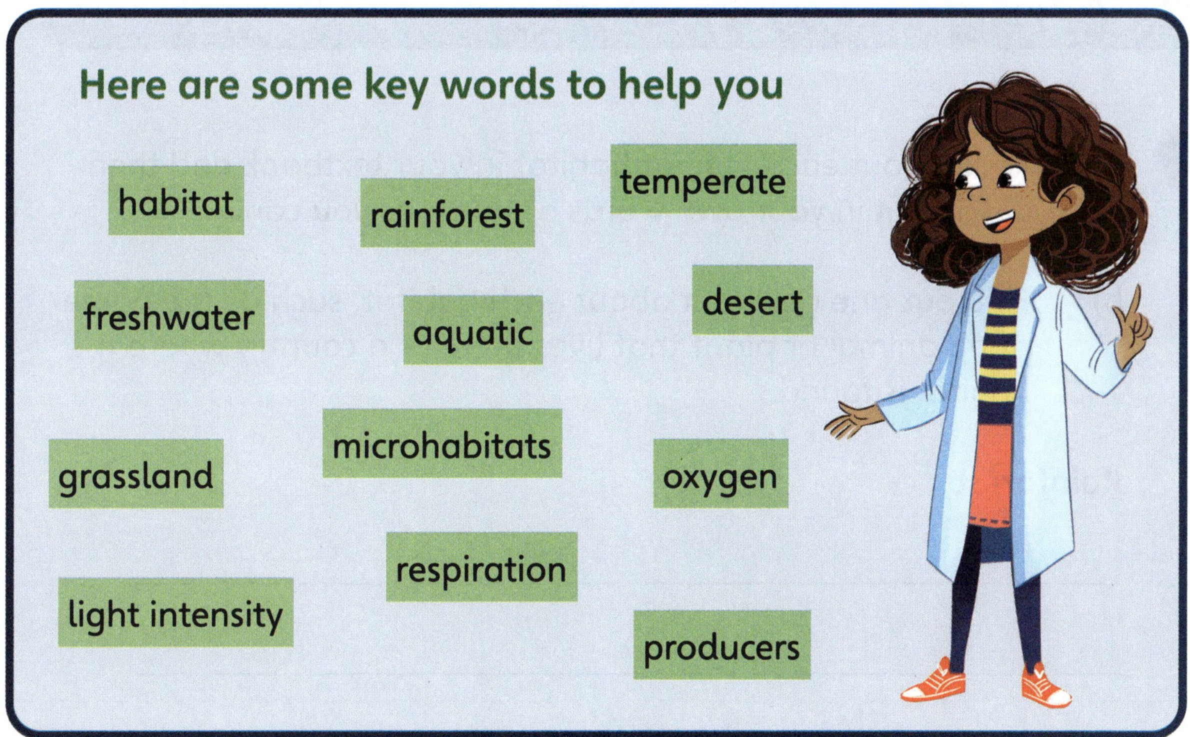

Choose two key words from the box above.
Write or draw what they mean.

Habitats around the world

1 a) Read about each type of habitat in your textbook and then describe it in your own words as much as you can.

b) Find out **one** new fact about each habitat, such as the name of an animal or plant that lives there or a country where the habitat is found.

Rainforest

____

____

____

____

Temperate forest

____

____

____

____

Oceans and seas

____

____

____

____

Freshwater ponds and lakes

____

____

____

Desert

____

____

____

Grassland or savanna

____

____

____

2 Find out about **one** more habitat. Name it and describe it.

____

____

____

Microhabitats

1 a) What does the word **habitat** mean?

____

____

b) What do scientists call the smaller places that differ in some way to the bigger habitat?

____

2 Name **two** things this plant can get in the crack that it cannot get on the path.

1. _______________________________

2. _______________________________

3 Why does this rainforest plant grow better on a tree branch than on the ground?

____

____

____

4 Circle **two** words that best describe the habitat of the small plants growing on the ground.

hot   cool   aquatic

shady   windy   desert

5 Look at a habitat outdoors where you live. Find a sunny part and a shady part.

Measure the light intensity, the temperature and how wet the soil is in both parts. Observe anything you cannot measure.

a)   What is causing the shade?

____

b)   Name the equipment used to measure:

    (i)   light intensity   _____________________

    (ii)   temperature   _____________________

c)   (i)   Write your measurements and observations in the table.

    (ii)   Write the type of habitat at the top.

Type of habitat:		
	Sunny part	**Shady part**
Description of place		
Light intensity		
Temperature		
How wet is it?		
Other observations		

Plants need water

1 a) What type of plant is shown in the picture?

____

b) Circle **two** words that describe this plant's habitat.

cold   hot

dry   wet

c) Why does this plant have spines instead of leaves?

____

2 a) Name the part of this plant that stores water.

____

b) Name the part of this plant that takes in water from the soil.

____

3 Draw **two** arrows on this picture to show two different places where water leaves the plant and enters the air.

4 This tree is called a mesquite tree.

  a) Name the type of habitat that it is growing in.

   ____

  b) Mesquite trees take in water from very deep underground.

   Predict what the underground part of this tree looks like.

   Draw your prediction.

5 This plant has very wide roots.

   Explain how the roots help the plant to survive in sandy soil.

   ____

   ____

   ____

Plants need oxygen

1   a)   Circle **one** place where air enters our body when we breathe.

     b)   (i)   Which gas in the air do we use to stay alive?

       ____

       (ii)   For which life process do we use this gas?

       ____

       (iii)   Name **one** place that our blood takes this gas.

       ____

2   Explain why leaves have very tiny holes like this.

____

____

3   Look at this plant. It was watered too much.

     a)   What has happened to the plant?

       ____

     b)   Which part of the plant is inside the pot?

       ____

     c)   How does too much water affect the air in the soil?

____

____

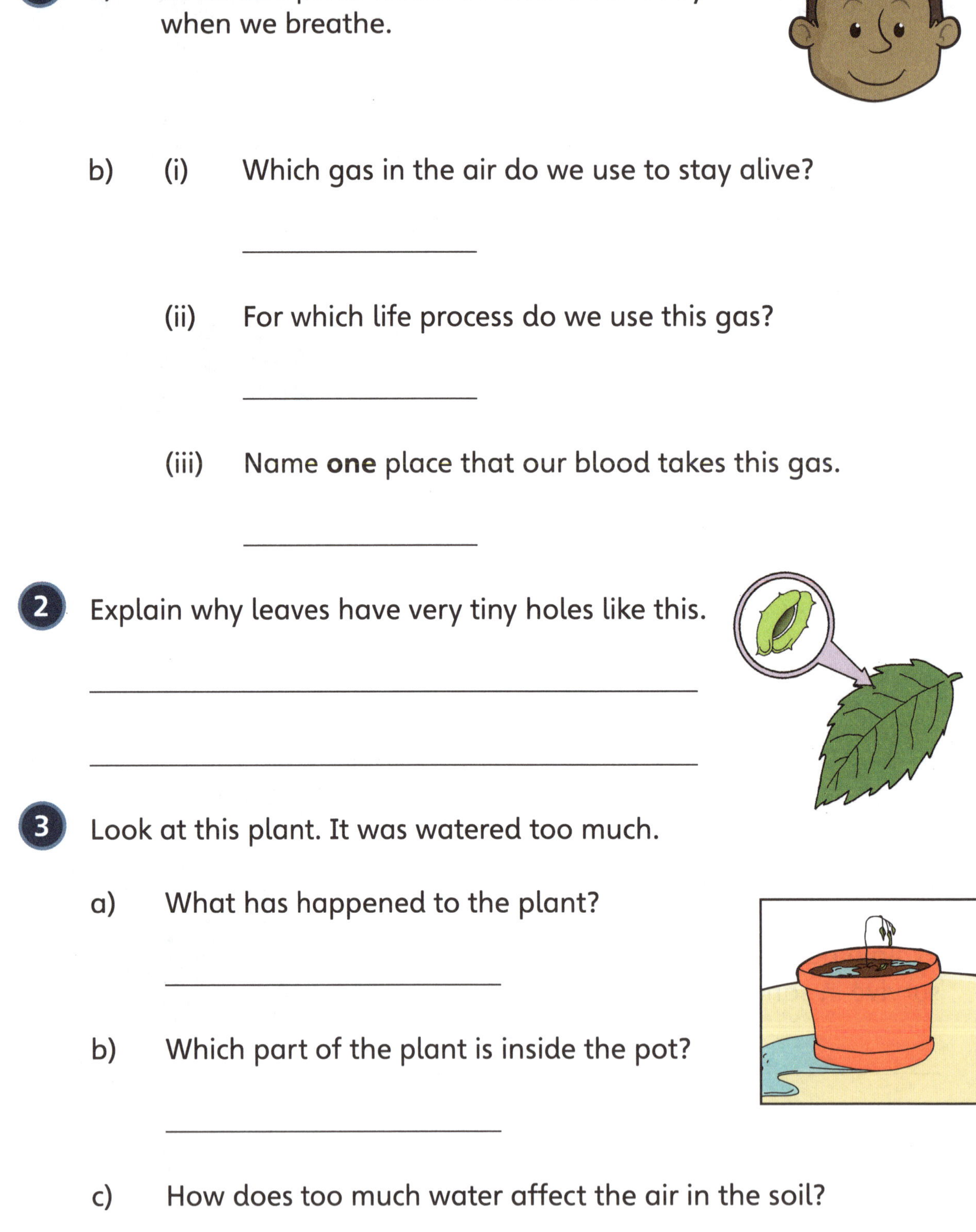

4 a) What type of plants are these?

____

b) Label these **four** parts of the plant by drawing a line and writing the word each time.

leaves   branch   trunk   root

c) Explain why this plant has some roots that are not in the soil.

____

____

____

Plants need light

1 a)   In which place do plants get **most** light? Circle **one** letter.

b)   Name the equipment used to measure light intensity.

____

c)   How are these plants getting more light than plants outside?

____

____

d)   How are these plants getting more light?

____

____

2 Green plants make their own food.

Circle **one** name for them.

consumers   producers   herbivores   predators

3 Write **one** word in each of the spaces **1**, **2** and **3** on the diagram to show what plants need to make food.

1. ___________

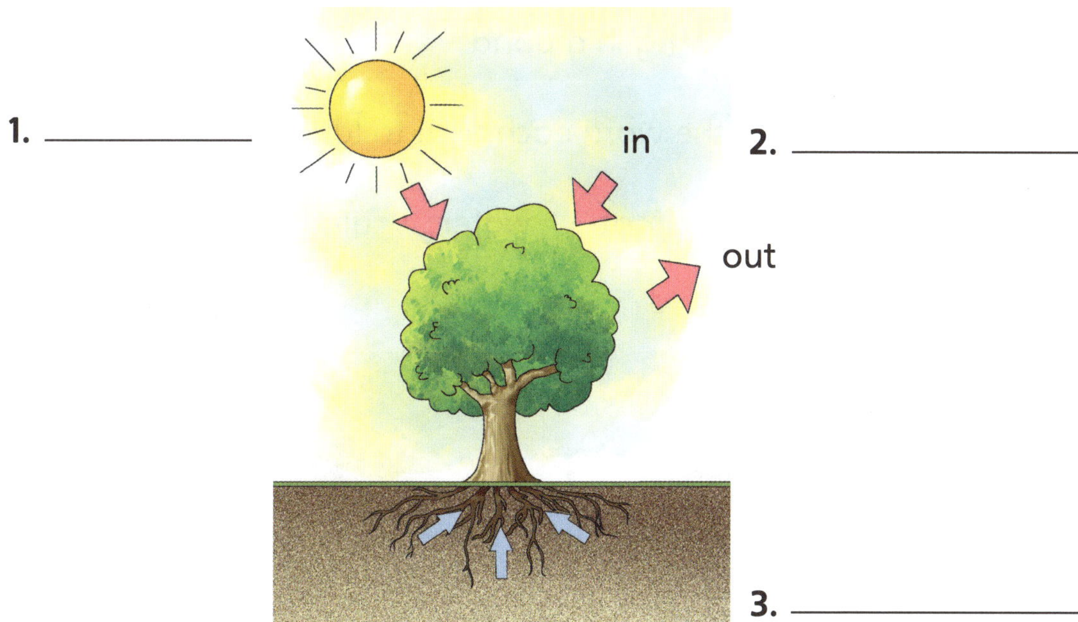

2. ___________

3. ___________

4 The pictures show how leaves grow on two different types of tree.

Picture A   **Picture B**

a) Explain why it is so dark under the trees in **Picture A**.

____

____

____

b) Explain why other plants grow well under the trees in **Picture B**.

____

____

Freshwater plants

1 a) This plant is growing in a pond.

Use a line and the word each time to label:

leaf   flower   root   water   air   soil

b) Circle **two** words to describe a pond habitat.

aquatic   dry   freshwater   ocean   salty

c) Explain why this plant only needs **small** roots.

____

____

2 This plant also grows in a pond.

a) What is the function of a plant's leaves?

____

____

b) These leaves do not overlap very much. How does this help the plant?

____

____

3 This flower grows above the water surface.

What is the function of a plant's flowers?

____

____

4 This pond plant has thorns on its leaves to stop them from being eaten.

a) Circle **one** living thing that eats leaves.

producer   predator

herbivore   carnivore

b) Explain what may happen to a plant if lots of its leaves are eaten.

____

____

Plants need minerals

1   a)   Which part of a plant takes in minerals from the soil?

       ____

   b)   Name **one** other thing that plants take in from the soil.

       ____

2   a)   What does this plant do to get more minerals?

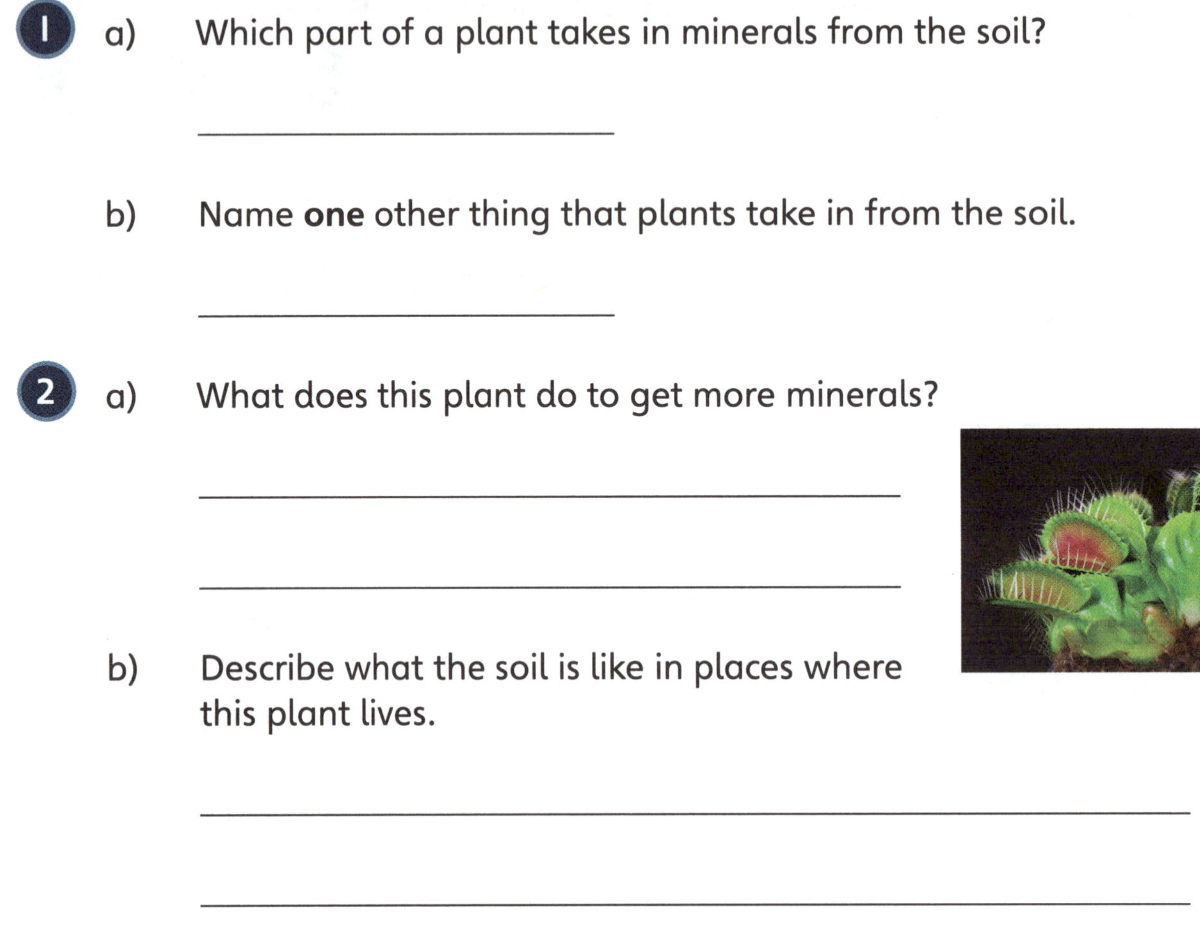

   b)   Describe what the soil is like in places where this plant lives.

3   These green plants do not have enough minerals.

   a)   Describe what has happened to each leaf.

(i)   ____

(ii)   ____

b)   This person is putting fertiliser into the soil.

Explain what fertiliser does.

____

____

c)   The next year, the person puts more fertiliser into the soil.

Suggest why the soil needs more fertiliser after one year.

____

____

4   Complete the sentences to describe how this plant gets extra minerals.

The plant has a smell that _____________________ insects.

When an insect goes inside the plant it cannot get _________________.

This is because the sides of the plant are _________________.

The insect falls into the _________________ that is inside the plant.

The plant breaks down the insect's _________________ and uses

the _________________ in it.

Comparing habitats

Choose **two** habitats to compare. Visit them if you can.

If not, then compare **two** habitats by doing your own research.

Name of habitat 1:

How does **habitat 2** differ from **habitat 1**? Is anything similar?

Name of habitat 2:

Predicting habitats

Plants in different habitats need different types of leaf and stem.

1 Draw the leaves of these three named plants.
Choose a fourth plant and draw its leaves. Write the name of the plant above your drawing.

Water lily	**Cactus**
Succulent	____________________

2 Draw the stems of these three named plants.
Choose a fourth plant and draw its stem. Write the name of the plant above your drawing.

Water lily	Palm tree
Long grasses	

What have I learned?

1 I understand that different habitats and microhabitats have different environmental conditions.

I know this because I can circle **two** words to describe a rainforest habitat.

aquatic   wet   dry   warm   cold   snowy

2 I understand that plant roots take in water and that the availability of water may affect root growth.

I know this because I can describe the roots of these plants.

water lily:

____

____

mesquite tree:

____

____

3 I understand that both plants and animals need oxygen from the air for respiration.

I know that muscles need _______________________ for respiration so they can contract.

4 I understand that plants need light and that the availability of light affects where they can grow.

I know that plants need enough light to make their

_______________________.

5 I can describe ways that plants are adapted to the environment they live in.

I know this because I can write **two** features of cacti.

1. ____

2. ____

6 I can compare plant adaptations in **two** contrasting habitats.

I know this because I can draw a pond plant and a succulent.

pond plant	succulent

7 I can predict the likely habitats of a variety of plants by looking at the adaptations they show.

I know this because I can predict the habitat of each of these plants.

Living things in danger

Habitats may change and this can sometimes be dangerous for living things. As the number of humans in the world increases, people want more land to grow crops or build homes. Other living things may lose their habitat when this happens. Some animals are endangered because humans want to take their horns or fur.

In this topic we will learn:

- that environments can be changed in ways that harm living things

- that environments can be changed in ways that help living things

- to recognise ways in which living things and the environment need protection, both locally and globally

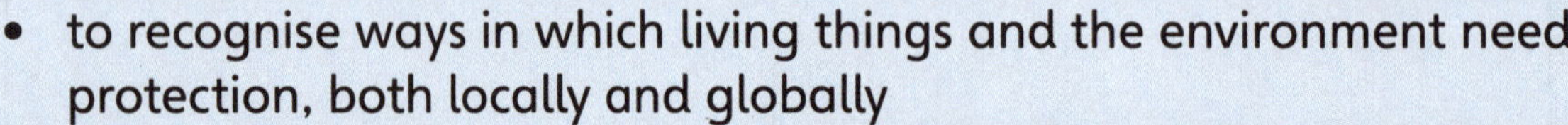

- about conservation and how to describe ways in which humans can reduce the effects of environmental change

- to describe what the terms *endangered* and *extinct* mean

- to explain how fossils are formed when things that have lived, or parts of living things, are trapped within rock

- how fossils provide evidence of organisms that are now extinct.

Choose two key words from the box above.
Write or draw what they mean.

Deforestation

1   a)   Describe what is happening in this picture.

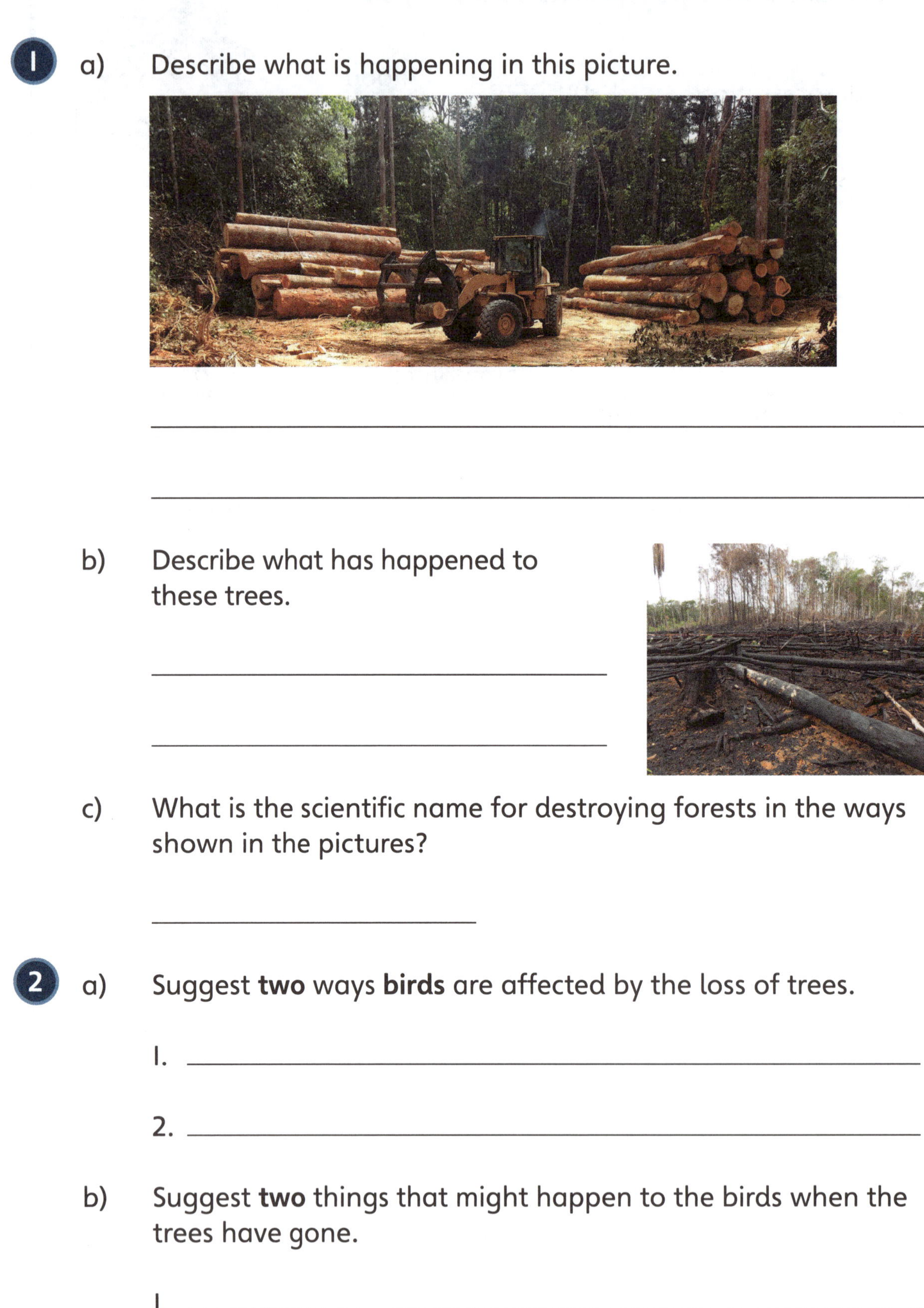

b)   Describe what has happened to these trees.

c)   What is the scientific name for destroying forests in the ways shown in the pictures?

2   a)   Suggest **two** ways **birds** are affected by the loss of trees.

1.

2.

b)   Suggest **two** things that might happen to the birds when the trees have gone.

1.

2.

c) Name another sort of animal that might be affected by loss of trees.

____

3 a) Suggest **two** reasons why people might cut down large parts of a rainforest.

1. ____

2. ____

b) (i) Slash and burning of forests puts extra minerals into the soil. What can people now grow there?

____

(ii) What happens when all the extra minerals are used up?

____

4 a) Find out more about a place in the world where there is a lot of deforestation. Write about it in your own words.

____

____

____

____

b) What do you think? Do you agree with humans cutting down forests? Give a reason for your answer.

____

____

____

Forest fires

1   a)   Use a line and the word to label **smoke** and **flames** on the picture of a forest fire.

b)   What sort of plants are burning in the picture?

____

c)   What is another name for these fires?

____

2   Koalas are herbivores that live in trees.

a)   Write **two** reasons why the koala needs trees in its habitat.

I. ____

2. ____

b)   Predict how these parts of a fire might harm a koala.

(i)   smoke: _______________________________________

(ii)   flames: _______________________________________

3 Forest fires and deforestation are different.

Draw **one** line from each statement to either **forest fire** or **deforestation**.

| Humans choose to cut down trees. |

| Trees burn then start to grow back again. |

forest fire

| Humans grow crops where trees once grew. |

| This happens in hot weather when grass is very dry. |

deforestation

| The forest trees are taken away for ever. |

4 Find out about how people can help to stop forest fires starting.

Write some ways.

____

____

____

____

Problems with water

1. The picture shows a house and some trees by a river.

a) Predict what this picture might look like if there is lots of rain and the river floods. Draw your prediction.

b) Small mammals and birds may live here.

Suggest what might happen to them if there is a flood.

small mammals: _______________________________

____

birds: ____

2 A big new road is going to be built where the dotted lines (....) are shown on the picture.

a) How will the new road affect animals living in the forest?

____

____

b) These animals are crossing a road.

(i) Suggest what could happen to them.

____

____

(ii) Compare how quickly they can cross the road.

____

____

____

c) Animals need water to drink.

Write **one other** reason that **amphibians** need water.

____

Helping animals to survive

1 Suggest what these ducks are crossing a road to find.

____

2 a) Draw a dotted line (....) on this picture to show the path for forest animals.

b) Suggest **one** reason why animals may want to walk along the path you have drawn.

____

c) What are paths like this called?

____

3 Describe how wildlife go to the other side of these roads.

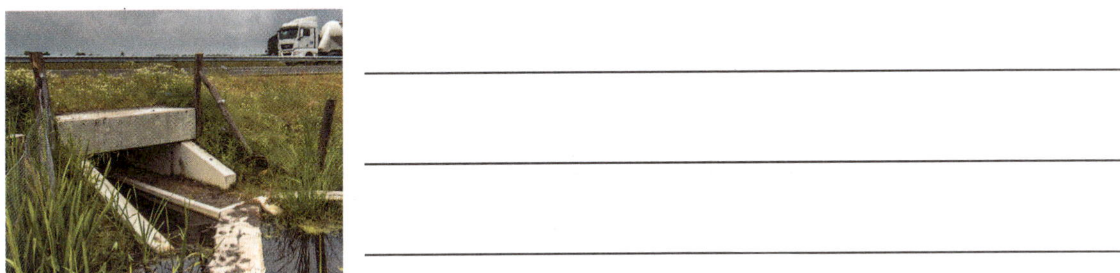

____

____

____

____

4 Describe what is helping this monkey to survive crossing a river.

____

____

Why protect living things?

1 What is the person in the picture doing?

____

2 Humans are trying to help giant pandas survive.

a) The table shows the number of giant pandas in the wild between 1974 and 2014.

Years	Number of giant pandas
1974–1977	2459
1985–1988	1114
1999–2003	1596
2011–2014	1864

(i) What was the **lowest** number of giant pandas?

(ii) In which year was the number of giant pandas **highest**?

____

(iii) What does *in the wild* mean? ________________________

____

b) The table shows the number of giant pandas in captivity in 2003 and 2014.

Year	Number of giant pandas
2003	164
2014	376

(i) What does *in captivity* mean? ________________________

____

(ii) Describe how the number of giant pandas in captivity has changed between 2003 and 2014.

____

c) Do you think humans are helping giant pandas to survive? Tick (✓) **one** box and give a reason for your choice.

Yes ☐　　No ☐

Reason: ____

____

3 Predict how this forest will change if all the trees are cut down.

List as many changes as you can.

____

____

____

____

Endangered species

1 Draw **one** line from each description to the correct scientific term.

The numbers of this species are so critically low that it is very close to becoming extinct.	●	●	endangered
There is no longer any of this species anywhere in the world.	●	●	critically endangered
There are very few of this species left. It is in danger of becoming extinct.	●	●	extinct

2 The Pinta giant tortoise became extinct in 2012.

Draw a picture of this giant tortoise and find out why it became extinct.

3 Choose one or more of these extinct birds.

dodo	moa	passenger pigeon	great auk

a) Draw or print out a picture of the bird you chose.

b) Find out why it became extinct and when.

Which species need our help most?

1 These animals are endangered or critically endangered. For each animal, find out:

- where it lives

- why it is in danger of extinction

- what is being done to help it.

Asian elephant:
endangered

Amur leopard:
critically endangered

eastern lowland gorilla:
critically endangered

green sea turtle:
endangered

Conservation

1 Complete the sentences by writing **one** word in **each** space.

A nature _________________ is a place where animals and plants are protected.

These places can also be called national _________________.

Protecting living things and their habitats is called

_________________.

2 a) (i) What is another name for criminals who steal from or kill animals?

____

(ii) What do they want to steal from this rhino?

____

b) Describe **one** way humans are trying to conserve rhinos.

____

____

3 a) Label a tusk on this elephant.

b) What material are tusks made of?

____

c) Describe **one** way humans are trying to conserve elephants.

____

____

4 Find out about conservation in places near where you live.
Make a fact sheet about an animal, plant or nature reserve that
interests you.

Animals from long ago

1. This is a fossil tooth. How long is the tooth?

   Use the scale under it to find out. _______________

2. These animals are extinct.

   a) What does *extinct* mean?

   ____

   b) Explain why we do **not** have any photographs of these animals.

   ____

3. This is a model of a fossilised animal.

   a) Name parts **A**, **B**, **C** and **D** on the answer lines on the next page.

    A ____

    B ____

    C ____

    D ____

b)   Explain why there is just a hole instead of an eye.

____

____

4 This is a fossil of an extinct animal.

a)   (i)   Suggest the habitat it once lived in.

    ____

    (ii)   Circle **one** piece of evidence on the picture to support your choice.

b)   Scientists think this animal ate other animals.

    Write **one** piece of evidence from the picture that supports this suggestion.

____

Evidence from fossils

1 Fossils usually form in this type of rock.

a) Name this type of rock.

____

b) What can you see in the picture above that can break some of these rocks?

____

c) The drawing shows three layers of this rock.
They are numbered **1**, **2** and **3**.

(i) Which number shows the **oldest** rock?

(ii) Circle **two** fossils showing animals that were alive at about the same time.

(iii) Scientists think that this rock was once under the sea. Describe **one** piece of evidence that supports this suggestion.

____

____

2 a) Use **Picture 1** and **Picture 2** to help you to explain how fossils are formed.

Picture 1

____

____

____

Picture 2

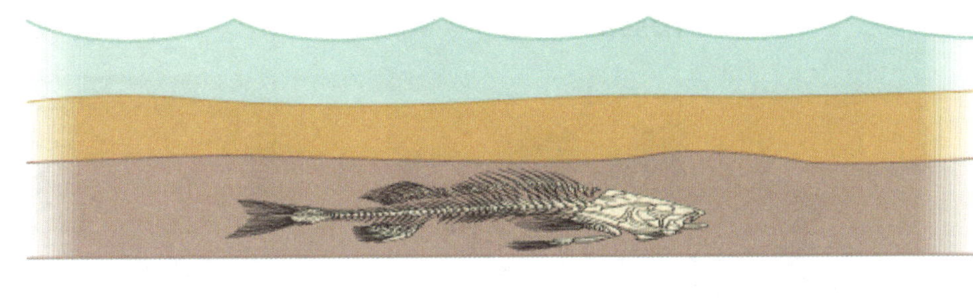

____

____

____

b) This diagram shows a fossil fish.

On the diagram, draw another fossil fish that lived **at the same time** as this one.

Other evidence from fossils

1 This is a fossil of part of a plant.

  a) Which part of a plant is it? _______________

  b) Suggest why scientists often find more vertebrate fossils than plant fossils.

  ____

  ____

2 The pictures show a fossil and a model of an extinct animal. The animal has features of a reptile and of a fish.

fossil   **model**

  a) Circle **two** parts of the animal that the fossil shows.

  head   tail   backbone   heart   eyes

  b) (i) Reptiles and fish have the same body covering. What is it?

  ____

  (ii) Describe **one** other way this animal is like a **reptile**.

  ____

  (iii) Describe **one** other way this animal is like a **fish**.

  ____

3 The diagram shows fossils in different layers of rock.

a) Which letter shows the **newest** rock?

____

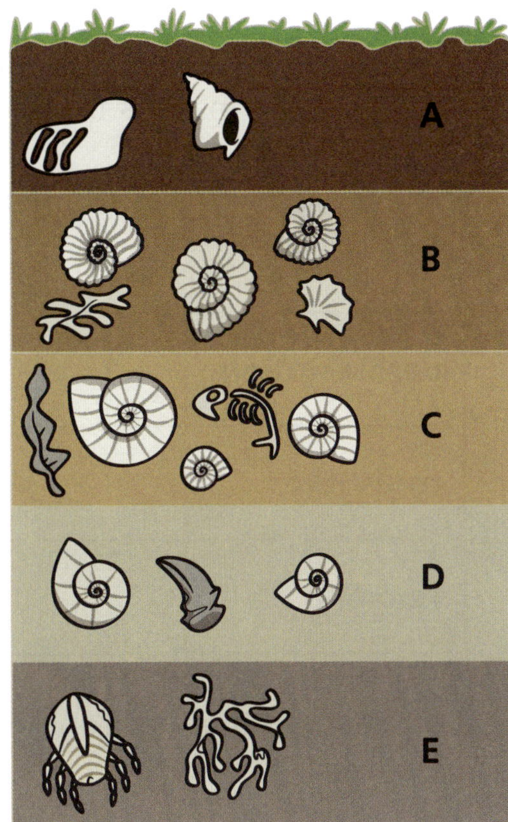

b) Draw **one** fossil of a living thing that was alive **before** this one.

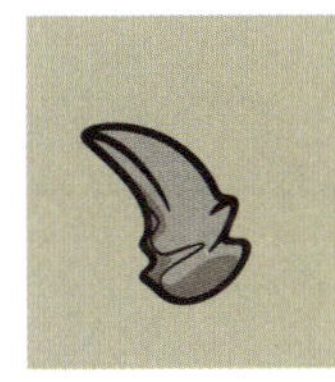

c) In which layer of the diagram is the **oldest** ammonite fossil? Write **A**, **B**, **C**, **D** or **E**.

____

d) Explain how ammonite fossils help scientists to predict the age of other fossils.

____

____

____

What have I learned?

1 I understand that environments can change and that this can sometimes be in ways that harm living things.

I know this because I can write **one** way each of these affects living things:

deforestation	
forest fires	
flooding	

2 I understand that environments can be changed in good ways that help living things.

I know this because I can describe what these are:

nature reserve	
wildlife corridor	

3 I can recognise ways in which living things and the environment need protection, both locally and globally.

I know this because I can state what poachers want to steal from these animals:

elephant	
leopard	
rhino	

4 I understand the term *conservation* and can describe ways in which humans can reduce the effects of environmental change.

I know this because I can describe **two** ways humans try to conserve animals.

1. ____

____

2. ____

____

5 I can distinguish between the terms *endangered* and *extinct* by writing their meanings in the table.

endangered	
extinct	

6 I can explain in simple terms how fossils are formed when things that have lived, or parts of living things, are trapped within rock.

I know this because I can show my teacher where I wrote about this in my workbook.

7 I understand how fossils provide evidence of plants and animals that are now extinct and information about when and where they may have lived.

I know this because I can describe what the diagram shows by completing the sentences.

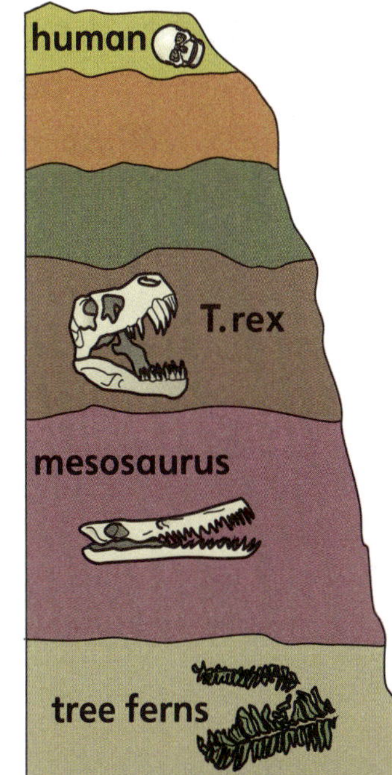

_______________________ are the oldest fossils.

_______________________ lived after mesosaurus.

There is evidence that T. rex ate _______________.

Diet and digestion

There are many different food types. A balanced diet contains the correct amount of food from a range of different food groups. Our digestive system breaks down the food we eat so that we can use it to give us energy to move and do things.

In this topic we will learn:

- that to stay healthy, humans need a balanced diet containing the correct amounts of a range of food groups

- about the relationship between diet, lifestyle, exercise and health

- about the sequence of processes of digestion in humans

- to describe the simple functions of the basic parts of the digestive system involved in the sequence of digestion.

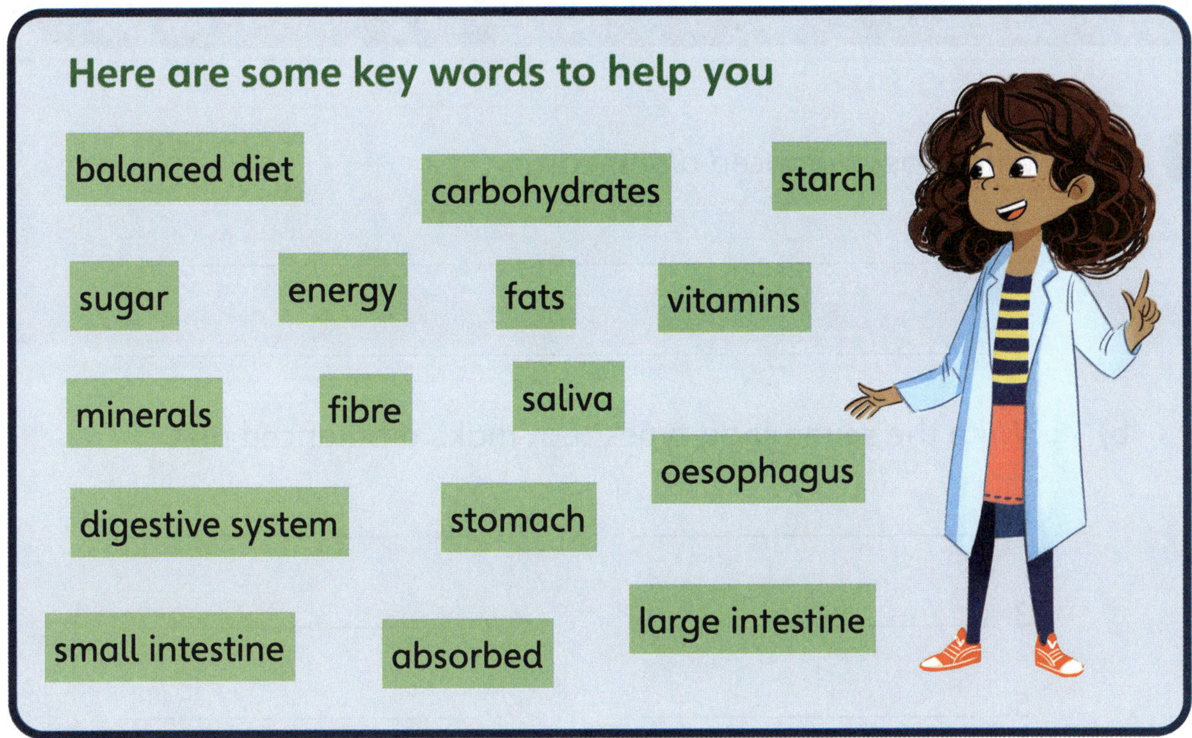

Choose two key words from the box above.
Write or draw what they mean.

Balanced diet

1 a) What does *balanced diet* mean?

____

____

b) Write the **seven** food types that make a balanced diet.

1. _______________   2. _______________

3. _______________   4. _______________

5. _______________   6. _______________

7. _______________

2 Use the pictures in your textbook to help with ideas for this question. You can choose other foods too.

a) Draw **two** different plates of food that you could eat regularly as part of a balanced diet.

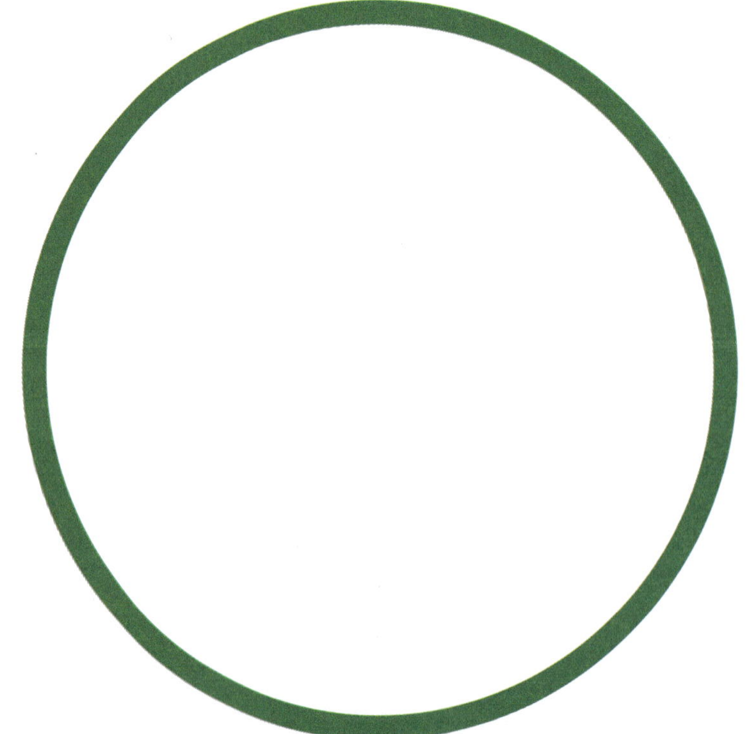

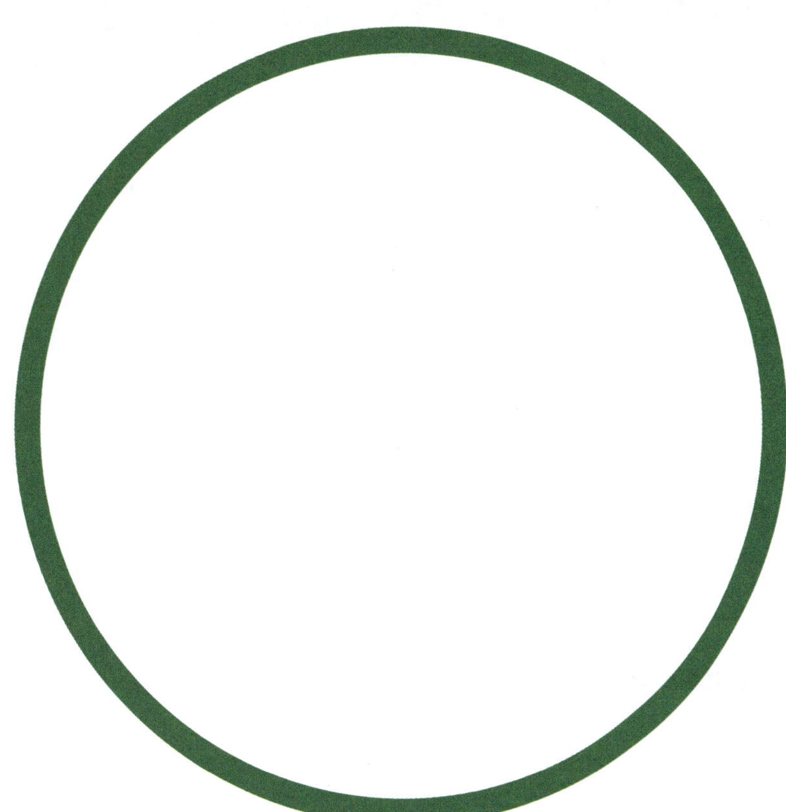

b) Draw **one** plate of less healthy food that you could eat sometimes, but **not** regularly.

Protein

1 a) Write **two** different foods that people with a **vegetarian** diet can get protein from.

   1. _________________________   2. _________________________

b) Write **four** other foods that contain a lot of protein.

   1. _________________________   2. _________________________

   3. _________________________   4. _________________________

c) Write **four** uses of protein in our bodies.

   1. _________________________   2. _________________________

   3. _________________________   4. _________________________

d) Why do we need to eat protein **regularly**?

   ____

2 Look at the six sources of protein in your textbook.

a) (i) Which **one** of those sources do you most like to eat?

   ____

   (ii) Find out which one other learners in your class chose. Write them in the tally chart.

b) (i) Use your results from part a) to complete the bar chart.

   (ii) How will you show a protein source that no one liked best?

   ____

Tally chart

Source of protein	Tally	Total

Bar chart

- Make each bar two squares wide. Draw them accurately.

- Write the names of the groups under the bars.

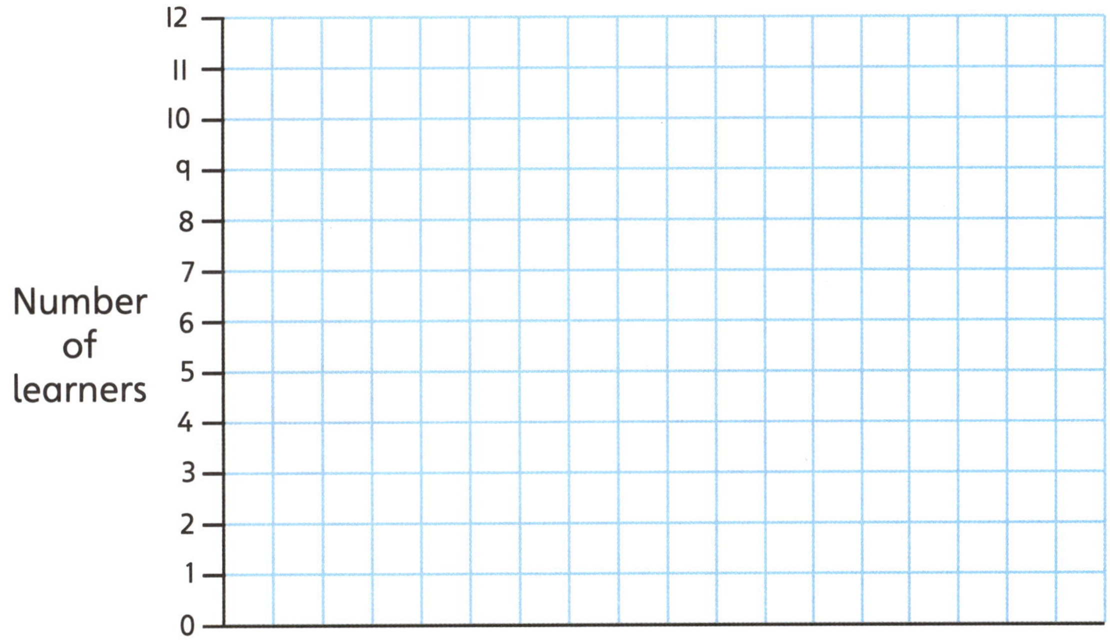

c) Which source of protein did most people like best?

____

Carbohydrate

1 a)   Name the source of carbohydrate shown in each picture.

b)   Circle the **starchy** carbohydrates.

Put a cross (**✗**) next to the **sugary** carbohydrates.

____

____

____

____

____

____

____

____

2   a)   How do our bodies use each of these types of carbohydrate?

Sugary carbohydrate

____

Starchy carbohydrate

____

b)   Find out how sugary food affects our teeth.

____

3   A learner draws this to represent **sugars**.

sugars

a)   Draw how she could represent **starch**
     using the same shapes.

b)   Explain why it takes longer to get energy from starch than
     from sugar.

____

____

Fat

1 a)   Name the source of fat shown in the picture.

____

b)   Name these two oils.

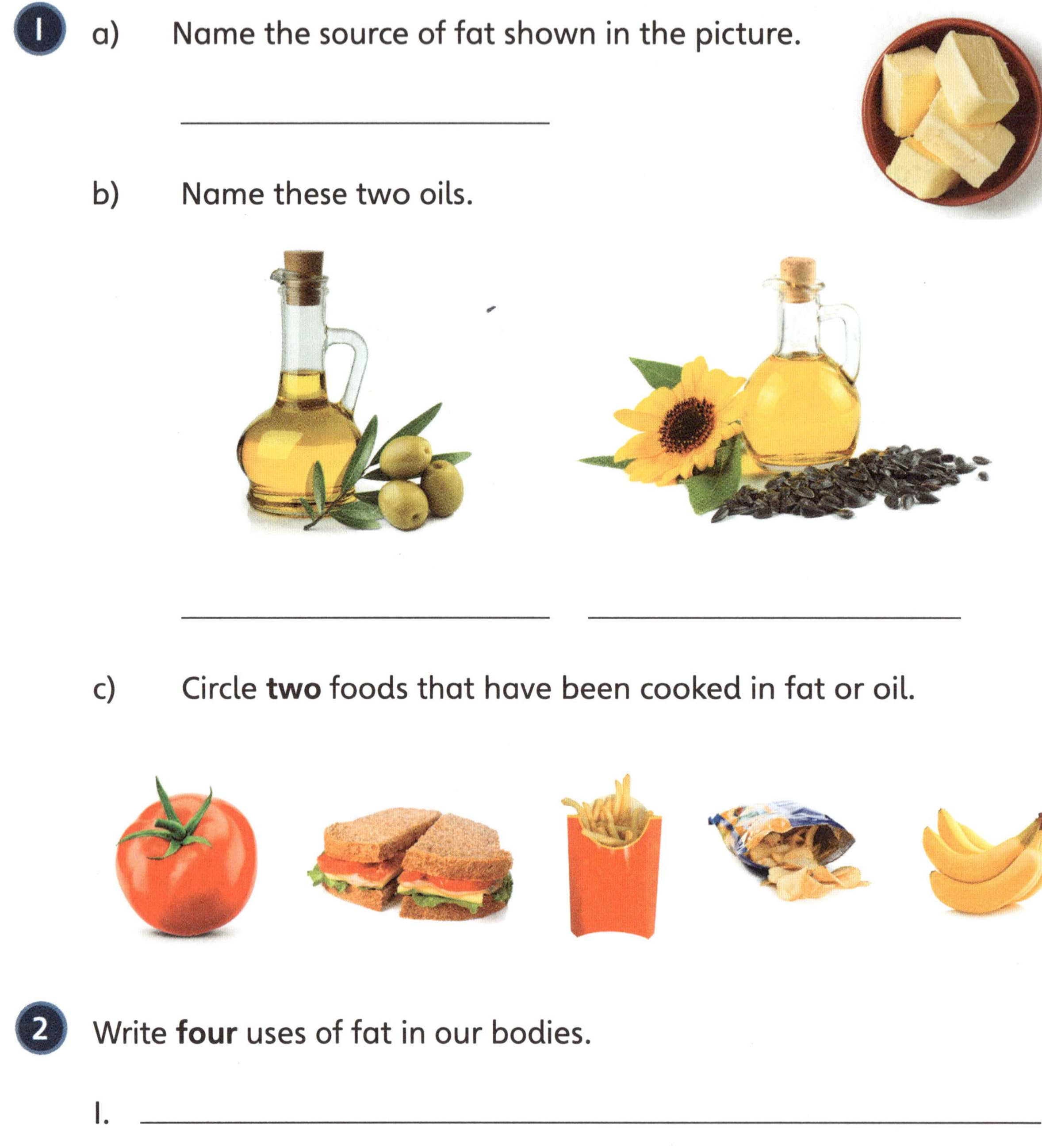

_______________________   _______________________

c)   Circle **two** foods that have been cooked in fat or oil.

2   Write **four** uses of fat in our bodies.

1. ____

2. ____

3. ____

4. ____

3 Finish this diagram to show some sources of fats and oils.

Add **at least four** more sources.

Minerals

1. Living things need minerals.

    a) Why do plants need minerals?

    ____

    b) Why do humans need minerals?

    ____

2. a) Why do humans need the mineral **calcium**?

    ____

    b) Name **one** calcium source that a person who **cannot** eat **dairy** food could eat.

    ____

    c) Name **two other** foods that are good sources of calcium.

    I. _______________________   2. _______________________

3. a) Why do humans need the mineral **iron**?

    ____

    b) Name **one** iron source that a person who **cannot** eat **eggs** could eat.

    ____

    c) Name **two other** foods that are good sources of iron.

    I. _______________________   2. _______________________

4 The table shows the amount of calcium that children of different ages need each day.

Age in years	Daily calcium in mg
Under 1 year	525
1 to 3	350
4 to 6	450
7 to 10	550
11 to 18 girls	800
11 to 18 boys	1000

a) Which age group needs **most** calcium each day?

____

b) How much daily calcium does a 5-year-old need?

____

c) Where do babies aged under 1 year get the calcium they need? Think about what they drink.

____

d) (i) How much daily calcium does a child who is the same age as you need?

____

(ii) Work out how much **more** daily calcium you will need when you are 11 to 18 years old than you do now.

Show the sum you do.

Answer: _______________ mg

1 a)   Why do humans need vitamins?

____

   b)   How much do humans need of each vitamin?

____

2 a)   Why do humans need vitamin **C**?

____

   b)   Name **three** foods that are good sources of vitamin **C**.

      1. _______________________   2. _______________________

      3. _______________________

3 a)   Why do humans need vitamin **A**?

____

   b)   Name **two** foods that are good sources of vitamin **A**.

      1. _______________________   2. _______________________

4 a)   Which **mineral** does vitamin **D** help us to absorb?

      ____

   b)   Name **one** food that is a very good source of vitamin **D**.

      ____

5 A scientist asks this scientific question:

> **Are vitamins and minerals needed for rats to grow well?**

The scientist has two groups of six rats.

Group A has a diet with **no vitamins and minerals**.

Group B has the **same food as Group A**, but they also have **2 cm³ of milk** every day.

The scientist weighs the rats every day.

a) Why does the scientist use **more than one rat** for each diet?

____

b) (i) What does the scientist change in this investigation?

____

(ii) What does the scientist measure in this investigation?

____

c) Predict which rats will grow faster by ticking (✓) one box.

Group A ☐   Group B ☐

Give a reason for your choice.

____

d) Name **one** vitamin and **one** mineral found in milk.

vitamin: _________________________

mineral: _________________________

Fibre and water

1 Complete the sentences about fibre using some words from the box.

stopping	milk	open	nutrients	plants
waste	moving	break	down	

Fibre does **not** give us any of the _________________ we need.

We use fibre to keep food _________________ through our bodies.

We get fibre from eating parts of _________________ that we cannot

_________________ _________________.

Eating fibre regularly makes it easier to remove _________________
when we go to the toilet.

2 Describe the high fibre foods shown in the pictures.
Use your textbook to help.

____

____

____

____

____

____

____

____

____

3 a) Name **two** parts of a human body that contain a lot of water.

1. ________________________   2. ________________________

b) How does our body tell us that we need to drink water?

____

c) Athletes sweat after a race.
What does sweating help them to do?

____

d) (i) What keeps our body *hydrated*?

____

(ii) How does being hydrated help us at school?

____

4 a) Keep a tally of how often you drink water in a month.

Try to use the same size glass or bottle each time.

Days	Week 1	Week 2	Week 3	Week 4
Monday				
Tuesday				
Wednesday				
Thursday				
Friday				
Saturday				
Sunday				

b) Do you drink more water on some days of the week than others?

____

1 Eating a balanced diet and drinking water regularly can help us to stay healthy.

a) Describe other things we should do to stay healthy. Use the pictures and their titles to help you.

Exercise

____

____

____

____

____

Relaxing on your own

____

____

____

____

____

Playing with other people or with pets

____

____

____

____

Getting enough sleep

____

____

____

____

b)   Write about how **you** try to do each of these things.

____

____

____

____

Ingestion

I The picture shows a mouth.

a) Draw a line from each word to label **three** parts of it. Use a ruler.

tooth

lip

tongue

b) What is the function of teeth?

____

c) What is the function of the tongue?

____

d) (i) Name the liquid made in the mouth. _______________________

(ii) Write **two** functions of this liquid.

1. ____

2. ____

e) Circle the word that means *putting food into the mouth*.

egestion   digestion   ingestion   respiration

f) Circle the word that describes a soft ball of food leaving the back of the mouth.

chewing   digesting   salivating   swallowing

2 a) Circle the letter showing the **digestive** system.

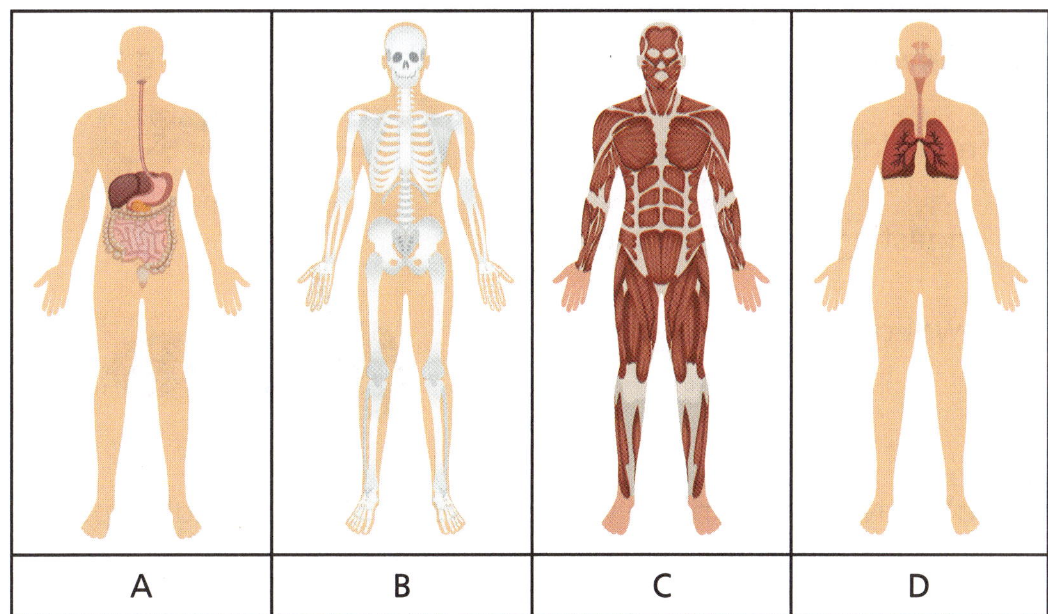

b) What is the function of the digestive system?

____

____

c) A learner draws a diagram to represent starch.

(i) Starch is chemically broken down in the mouth.

Draw a diagram to show what it looks like now.
Use the same shapes.

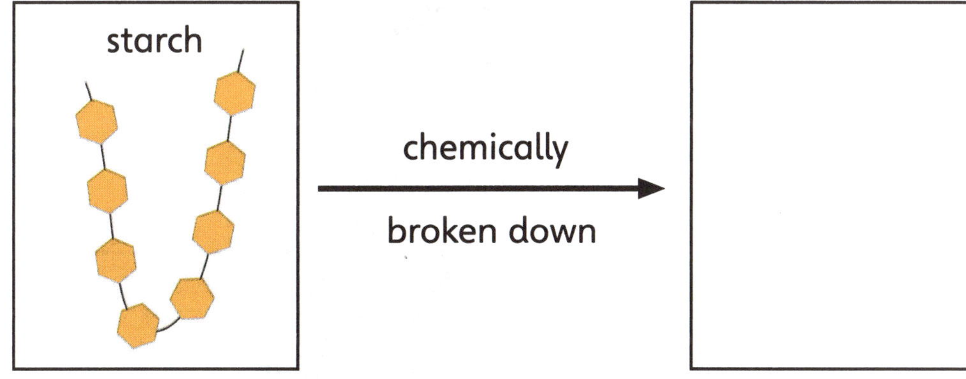

(ii) What is starch broken down into? Write the word above
your drawing.

Swallowing

1 Circle **two** words to describe what this snake is doing to a rat.

egesting   chasing

ingesting   listening

swallowing   sweetening

2 a)   Name **one** place where **physical** digestion takes place in humans.

____

b)   Describe how humans physically make food easier to swallow.

____

____

____

c)   Name the **three** parts of the digestive system shown with lines on this diagram.

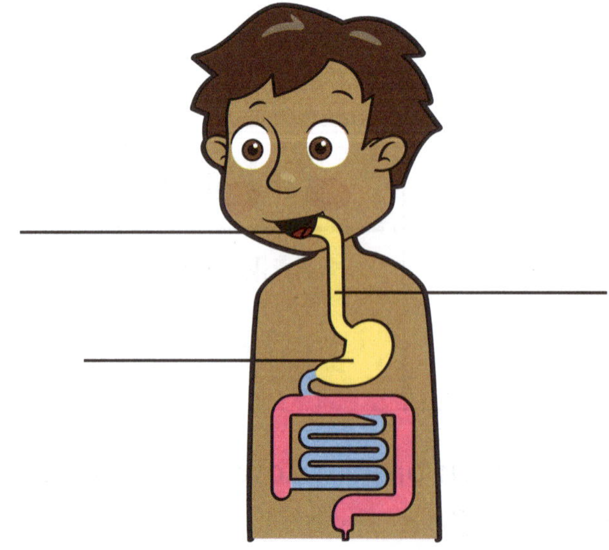

3 The diagram shows swallowing.

a) Draw a line from the words to label:

ball of food

oesophagus

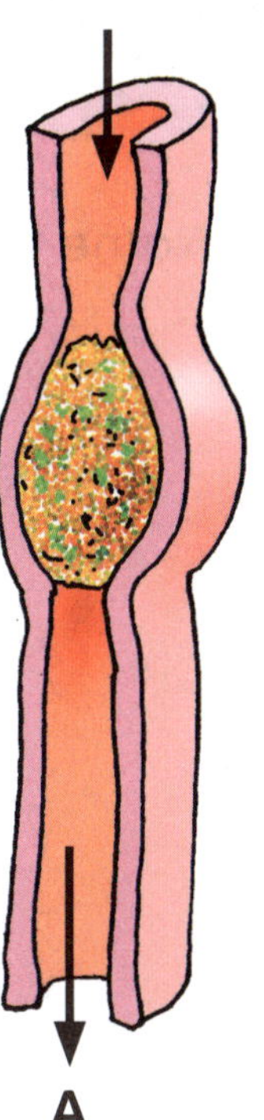

b) Where does the arrow labelled **A** show the
ball of food going to next?

____

c) (i) Write **contract** or **relax**
beside each label line to
show what the muscles are
doing.

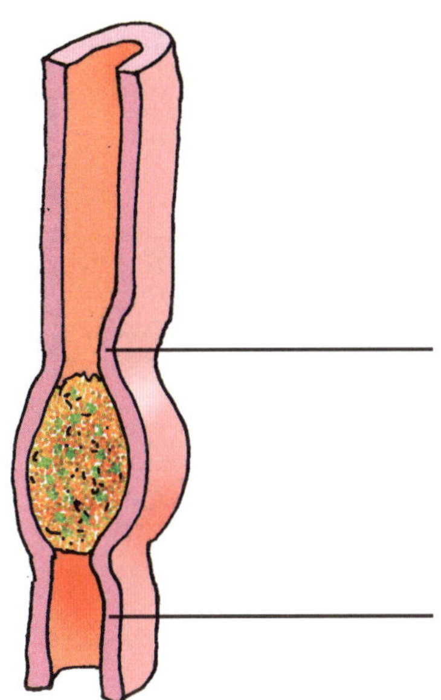

(ii) Describe what the muscles are doing to the ball of food.

____

Parts of the digestive system

1. Name the **six** parts of the digestive system shown by the lines.

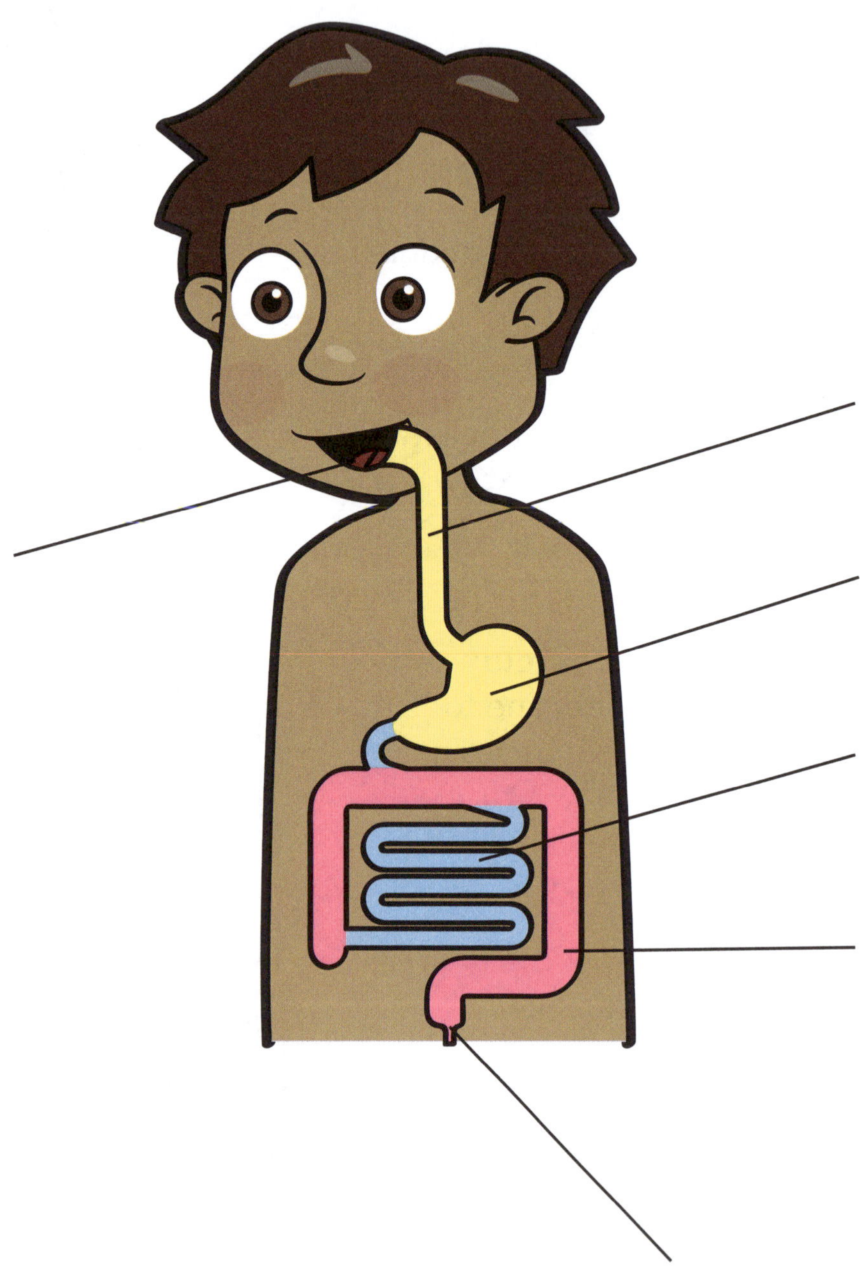

2 Describe what happens to food in each of these places.

stomach	
small intestine	
large instestine and anus	

A model of the digestive system

1 Complete the table by describing what each part of your model of the digestive system represents. Use your textbook to help.

Part of model	Part of digestive system
Crushing and grinding the banana and biscuits with water.	This represents physical digestion in the mouth. Crushing and grinding represents ______________________________ ______________________________. The water represents ______________.
The sealed bag with the food, water and orange juice in it.	The bag represents the ______________ with food and ______________ juices inside it. This is where ______________ takes place.
Shaking and squeezing the bag.	This represents the stomach ______________ the food to mix it with ______________ juices.
Putting the food from the bag into the stocking.	This represents the food moving from the ______________ into the ______________ intestine to complete digestion.

Part of model	Part of digestive system
Absorbing what comes out of the sides of the stocking.	This represents _____________ of useful materials from the small intestine into the _____________.
Pushing the food further along the stocking.	This represents the food moving from the _____________ intestine to the _____________ intestine.
Squeezing out any remaining liquid.	This represents water being _____________ from the food waste in the large _____________.
Squeezing food out of a hole at the end of the stocking.	This represents the waste food that is the _____________ in our diet being _____________ through the anus.

2 Suggest **one** improvement to your model.

____

____

1 a) What does the word *sequence* mean?

____

b) Write each of the **five** words in the correct place on the diagram to show the order in which they take place in the digestive system.

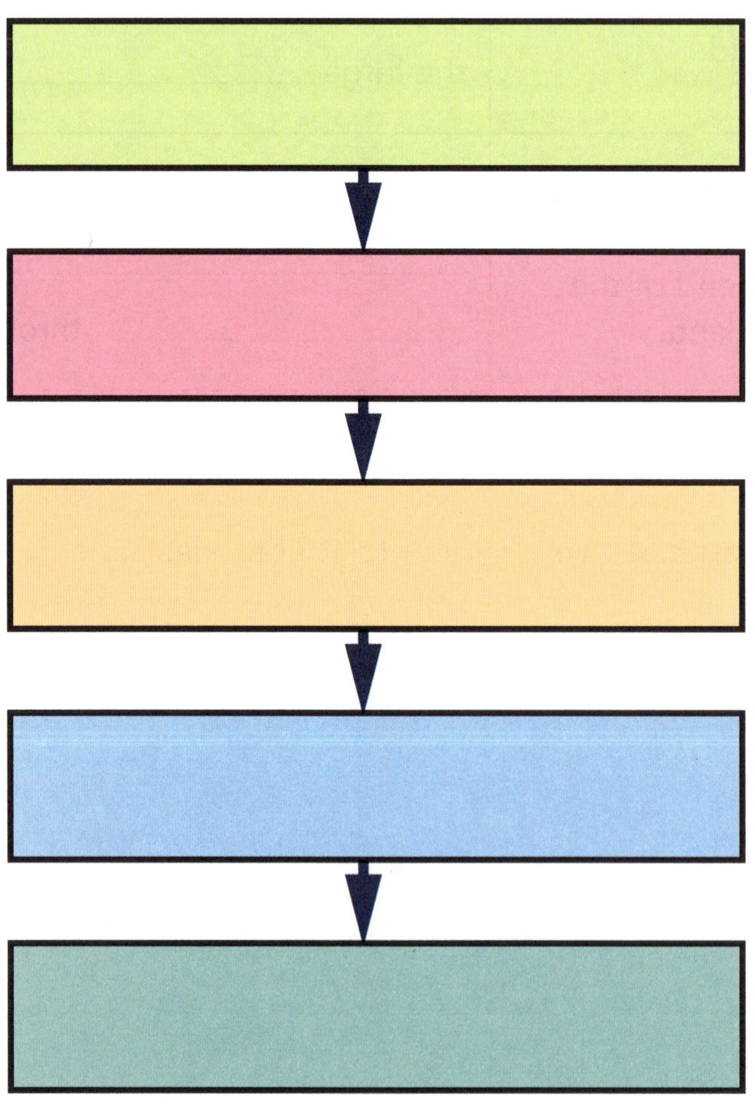

2 Draw **one** line from each part of the digestive system to what happens there. Some parts are shown in words, some are pictures.

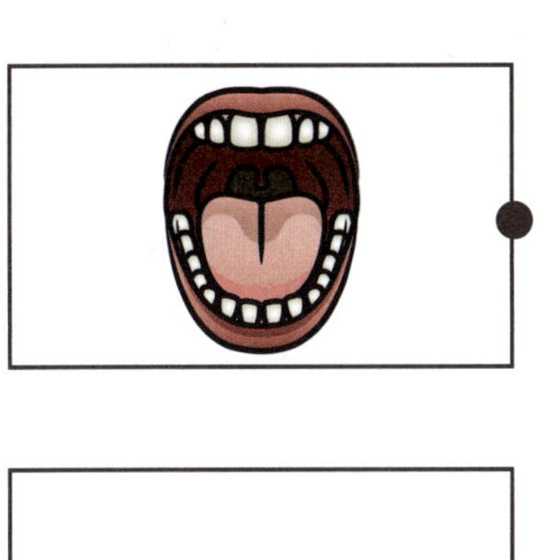

anus

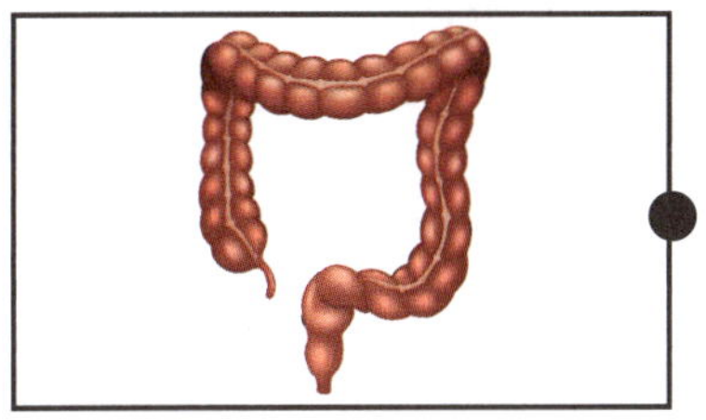

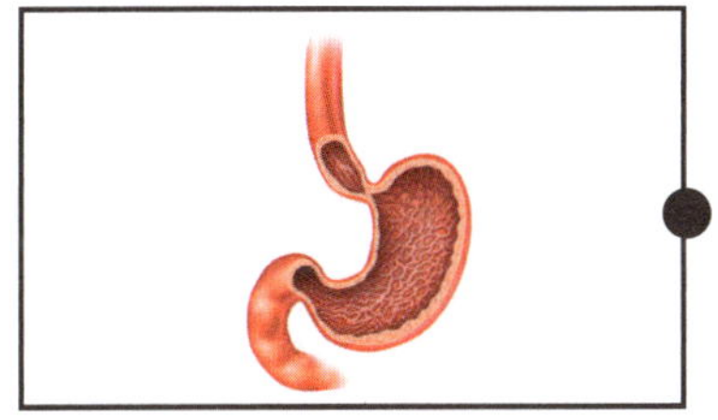

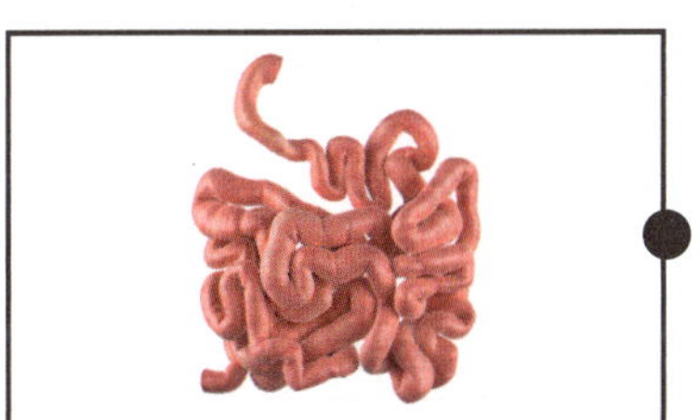

oesophagus

egestion of waste

absorption of **water** from waste

ingestion
+
physical digestion

swallowing

churning food
+
digestion of protein

completing digestion
+
absorption of **digested food** into the blood

1 I understand that to stay healthy, humans need a balanced diet containing the correct amounts of a range of food groups.

I can give examples from each food group and their function.

I know this because I can complete this table, which continues on page 79. One row is completed.

Food groups in a balanced diet	Two examples	One function of this food
water	1. tap water 2. watermelon	It keeps our body, blood and organs hydrated.
	1. 2.	
	1. 2.	
	1. 2.	
	1. 2.	

Food groups in a balanced diet	Two examples	One function of this food
	1. 2.	
	1. 2.	

2 I understand the relationship between diet, lifestyle, exercise and health.

I know this because I can show my teacher pages 66 and 67 of my workbook, which is where I wrote about this.

3 I can sequence the processes of digestion in humans.

I know this because I can number these processes in order, using numbers **1**, **2**, **3**, **4** and **5**.

swallowing	egestion	absorption	ingestion	digestion

4 I can describe the simple functions of the basic parts of the digestive system involved in the sequence of digestion.

I know this because I can show my teacher page 73 of my workbook, which is where I completed a table showing this.

Mixing and separating materials

There are different methods of separating mixtures. When larger solids are mixed with smaller solids they can be separated by sieving. Some solids, such as salt, dissolve in water. When a solid dissolves in water we must evaporate the water into the air to separate the solid again.

In this topic we will learn:

- that solids can be mixed, and that sieving may be used to separate some mixtures

- about how filtration may be used to separate some solids from a liquid

- that when a solid dissolves in water it forms a solution that cannot be separated by filtration

- to describe ways in which simple substances such as sugar and salt can be dissolved more quickly

- that when a solution is left with air around it the liquid will evaporate, leaving just the dissolved solid

- to use our knowledge of solids, liquids and gases to decide how to separate mixtures.

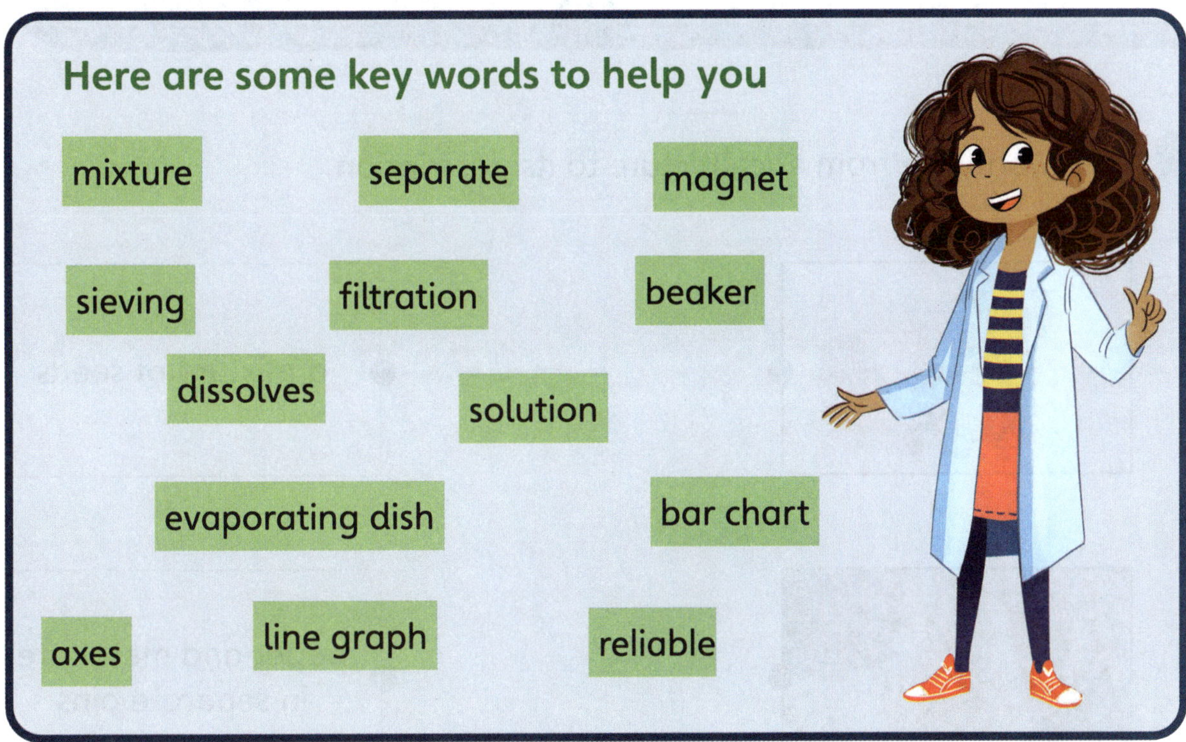

Choose two key words from the box above.
Write or draw what they mean.

Mixtures

1 Draw **one** line from each picture to its description.

a mixture of seeds

paper and metal are in separate bins

a mixture of sweets

different fruits are separated in a shop

these beans are in separate groups

2 a)   Name **equipment A**.

equipment A

____

b)   Circle all the materials that will be attracted to **equipment A**.

sand	steel	copper

iron	plastic	wood

c)   Explain how you could use **equipment A** to separate this mixture of sand and small pieces of iron.

mixture of sand and small pieces of iron

____

____

____

d)   Which of these mixtures could you separate with **equipment A**? Tick (✓) **one** answer.

salt and copper ☐   flour and rice ☐

copper and steel ☐   steel and iron ☐

Sieving

1 a) The picture shows flour and seeds.
Write **mixture** or **separated** by each label line.

b) Nadene puts the same mixture into a sieve.

(i) Write **mixture** or **separated** on each empty label line.

(ii) What is in the bowl?

____

c) Tick (✓) **all** the mixtures that can be separated with a sieve.

flour and raisins ☐

sugar and flour ☐

sand and sugar ☐

sugar and dried pasta ☐

nuts and flour ☐

2 Complete the sentences about sieving using words from the box.

Words may be used **more than once**.

size	smaller	larger	similar

Sieving can be used to separate a _______________ solid

from a _______________ solid. The _______________

solid stays in the sieve.

Sieving will **not** separate solids with grains of

_______________ _______________.

3 The holes in different sieves differ in size.

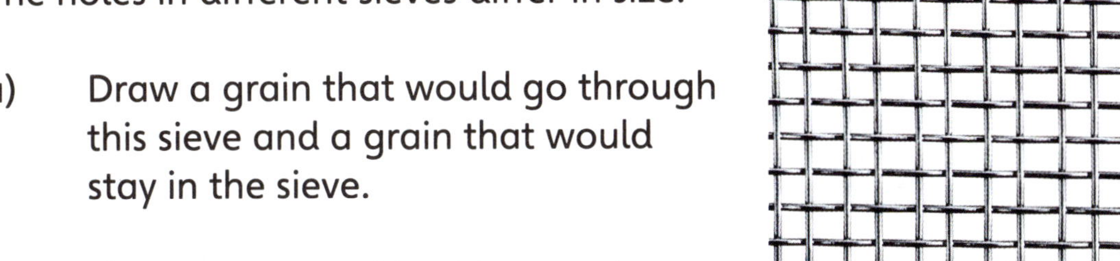

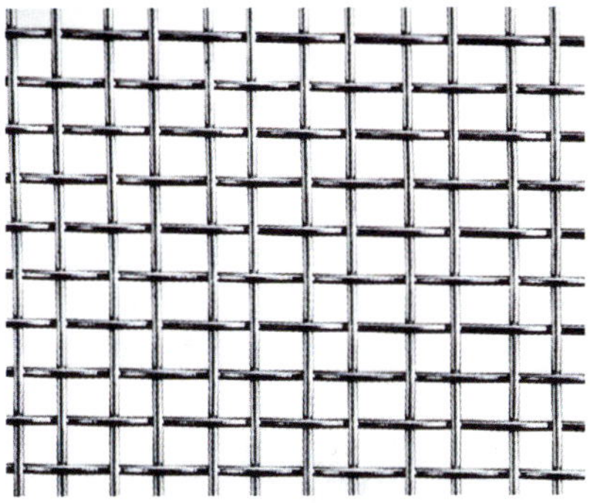

a)   Draw a grain that would go through this sieve and a grain that would stay in the sieve.

Draw the grains like this • on the picture.

b)   Milo uses this sieve to separate soil and stones.

Suggest why some of the stones and soil do **not** separate.

____

____

____

Filtration

1. The picture shows some sand and some water.

sand   **water**

   a)   Name the equipment the water is in.

   ____

   b)   Are these materials **solid**, **liquid** or **gas**?

   (i)   water   _______________________

   (ii)   sand   _______________________

2. This is a mixture of sand and water.

A learner wants to separate the sand from the water by filtration.

   a)   Name these pieces of equipment that she needs.

   (i) 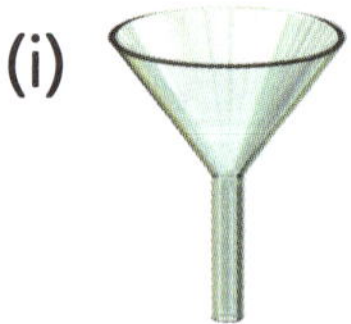   (ii) 

   _______________   _______________

   b)   Complete this sentence about filtration.

   Filtration can be used to separate a liquid from a

   _______________ that we can _______________.

3 a) The learner pours the sand and water into the equipment.

(i) Predict which material will stay in here.

____

(ii) Complete the diagram in (i) by drawing **one** more piece of equipment she needs.

Draw it in the correct place.

b) (i) Label **sand** and **water** on this diagram.

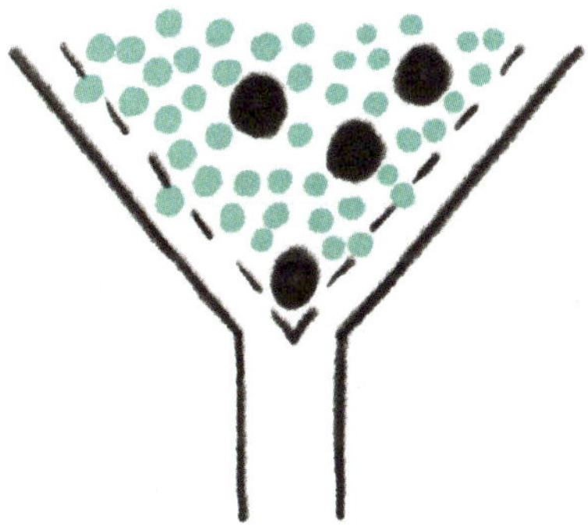

(ii) Justify* your prediction in a) (i) by describing what this diagram shows.

____

____

____

*Justify means to *show* that you are correct.

Drawing equipment

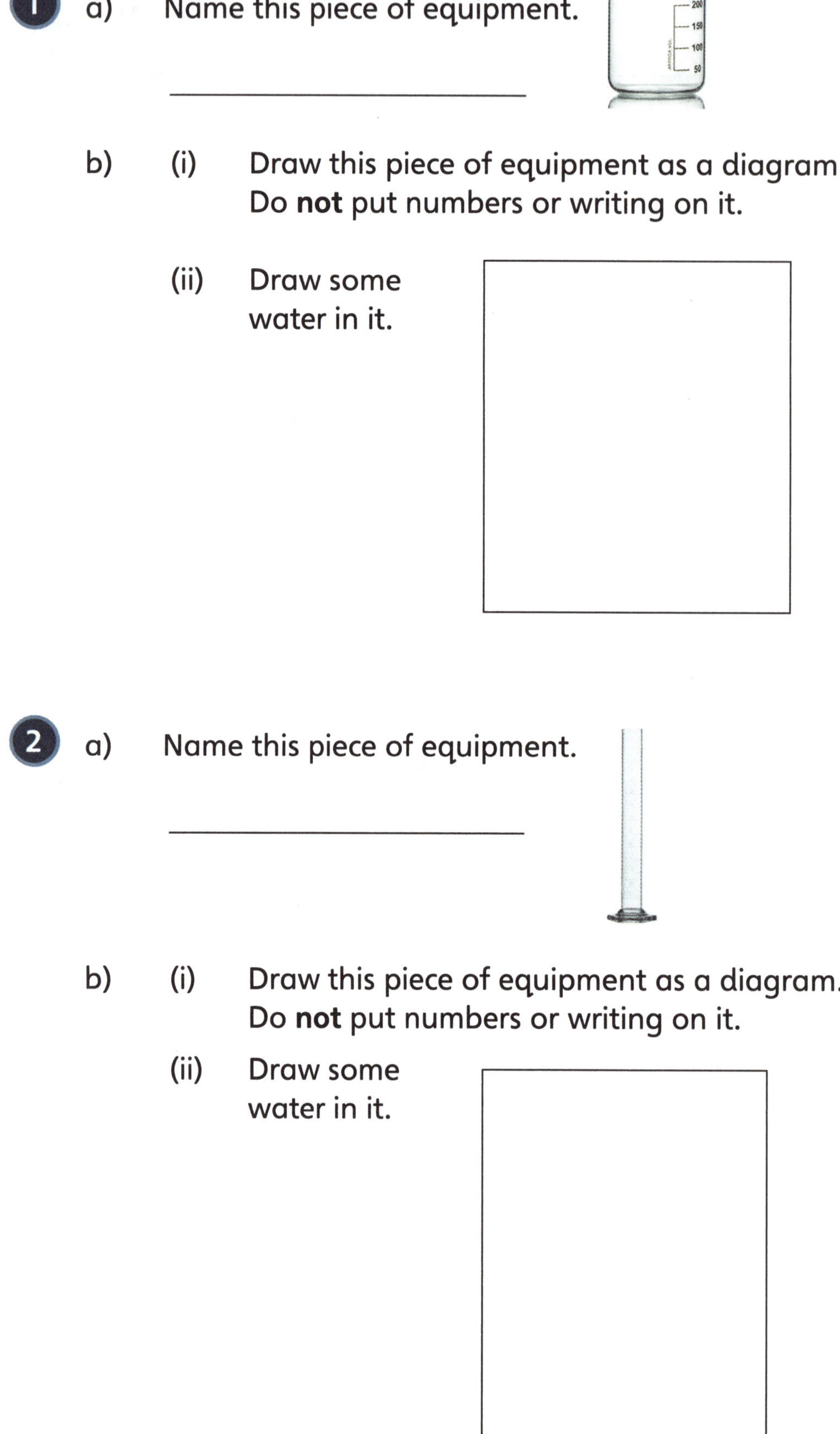

1 a) Name this piece of equipment.

____

b) (i) Draw this piece of equipment as a diagram. Do **not** put numbers or writing on it.

(ii) Draw some water in it.

2 a) Name this piece of equipment.

____

b) (i) Draw this piece of equipment as a diagram. Do **not** put numbers or writing on it.

(ii) Draw some water in it.

3 a)   Draw this equipment as a diagram.

     Do **not** use colour.

   b)   Draw **two** label lines and name both pieces of equipment on **your** diagram.

4 You may not have used this piece of equipment, but can you predict how to draw it as a diagram?

Try drawing it.

Dissolving

1 a) A teacher puts some salt into a pan of hot water.

He can no longer see the salt.

What has happened to the salt?

____

b) Why do splashes of sea water taste salty?

____

2 This beaker contains **sand**, **salt** and **water**.

a) Label these **three** materials using a line and the word each time.

b) What method of separating is this equipment used for?

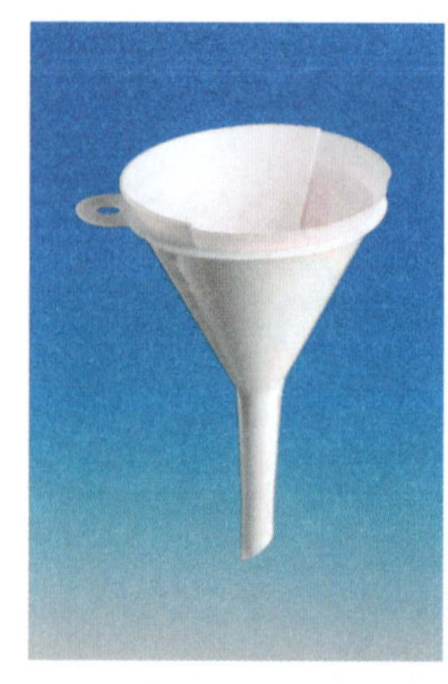

____

c)   A learner draws a diagram of her equipment.

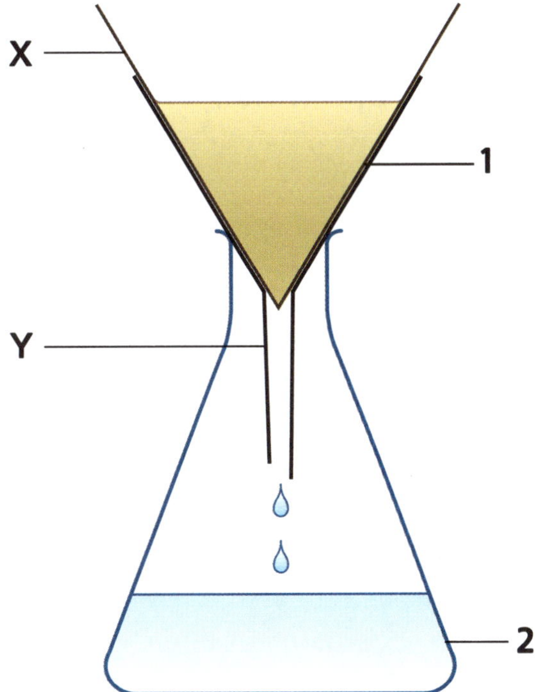

(i)   Name equipment **X**. _______________________

(ii)   Name equipment **Y**. _______________________

d)   She pours sand, salt and water into the top of the equipment.

(i)   Which of the materials stays in **1**?

____

(ii)   Name the contents of **2**.

____

e)   Circle **one** box to show materials that could also be separated
using this equipment.

iron and gravel	sugar and water
flour and sand	soil and water

Finding the dissolved salt

1 This beaker contains salt and water.

a) We cannot see the salt.

What has happened to it?

____

b) Draw a **labelled** scientific diagram of this beaker of salt and water in the space below.

c) A learner pours some of the liquid from the beaker into this equipment.

(i) Name this equipment.

____

(ii) Suggest a warm place where the learner could put the liquid now.

____

2   During the next lesson the learner looks at the equipment she put the liquid into.

This is what she sees.

a)   (i)   Complete the label to show what she sees.

(ii)   Where has what she sees come from?

____

____

b)   What has happened to the water?

____

c)   Circle **one** box to show materials that could also be separated using this equipment.

copper and gravel	sugar and water
salt and sugar	flour and sand

Dissolving faster

Answer these questions for **one** of the investigations (**A**, **B** or **C**) in your textbook.

1. Write your scientific question.

   ____

   ____

2. a) What is the **one** factor you will change?

   ____

   b) What will you measure?

   ____

3. Write a list of the equipment you will need.

   __________ __________ __________ __________

   __________ __________ __________ __________

4. a) What volume of water will you use? __________

   b) Which equipment will you use to measure this volume?

   ____

5. a) How will you decide when to stop the timer?

   ____

   b) How will you make sure that you observe each beaker in the same way?

   ____

   ____

6 Draw a labelled scientific diagram of each of your beakers.

7 a) Write the missing column heading for the factor you changed.

	Time it takes for sugar to dissolve in seconds

b) Write your results in the table.
Remember that the unit is already in the column heading.

8 Write a conclusion that answers your scientific question.

____

____

9 How could you improve your investigation?

____

____

Making a water filter

1 Draw and label your beaker of dirty water.
Draw it as a scientific diagram.

2 a) Label the layers in this water filter.

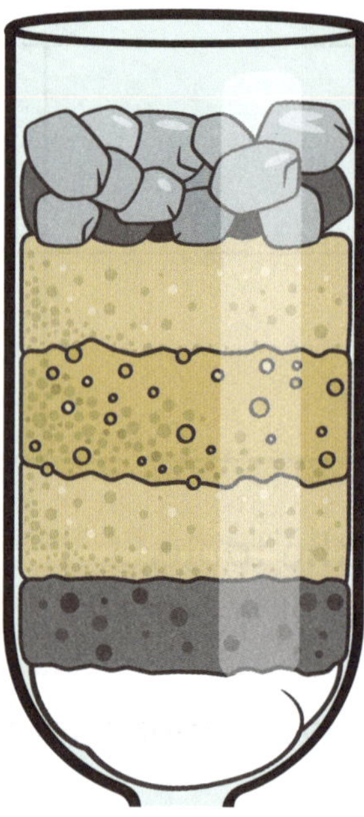

b) Describe any ways that your water filter differs from this one.

____

____

____

Answer these questions **after** you have used your water filter.

3 a) Was your water cleaner when it came out of the filter? Describe what it looked like.

____

____

b) Which layer trapped leaves? _______________________

c) Which layer has the largest air spaces for water to pass

through? _______________________

d) (i) Is the cotton wool dirty? Or was the water clean before it reached the cotton wool?

____

____

(ii) Which layer trapped the smallest particles of mud?

____

e) How could you find out whether your filtered water has salt in it? Write the equipment you need and what you would do.

____

____

____

____

f) Suggest any improvements you could make to your water filter.

____

____

Presenting results

I Look at this table.

Column A	Column B

a) In a results table, which factor is always written in **Column A**?

____

b) Which factor is always written in **Column B**?

____

c) Where are units written in a results table?

____

d) Look at this bar chart.

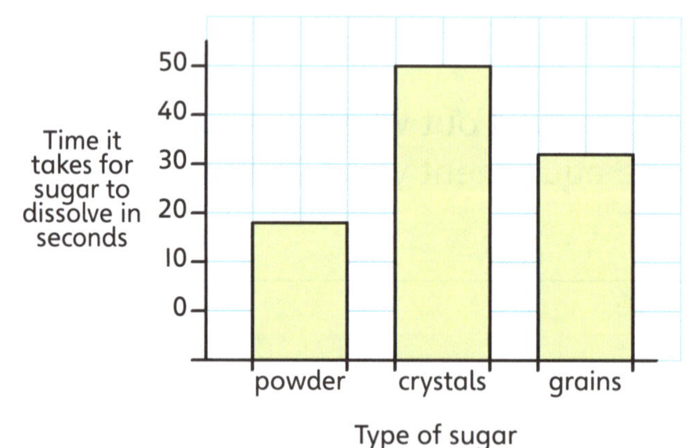

Write **A** or **B** in the answer spaces below.

(i) Which column of the results table has the information on the **horizontal** axis come from? ______

(ii) Which column has the information on the **vertical** axis come from? ______

2 a) The table shows the results of an investigation.

Water temperature in °C	Time it takes for a sugar cube to dissolve in seconds
20	130
30	110
40	94
50	50

Plot a **line** graph for these results.

Plot the points carefully with a sharp pencil.

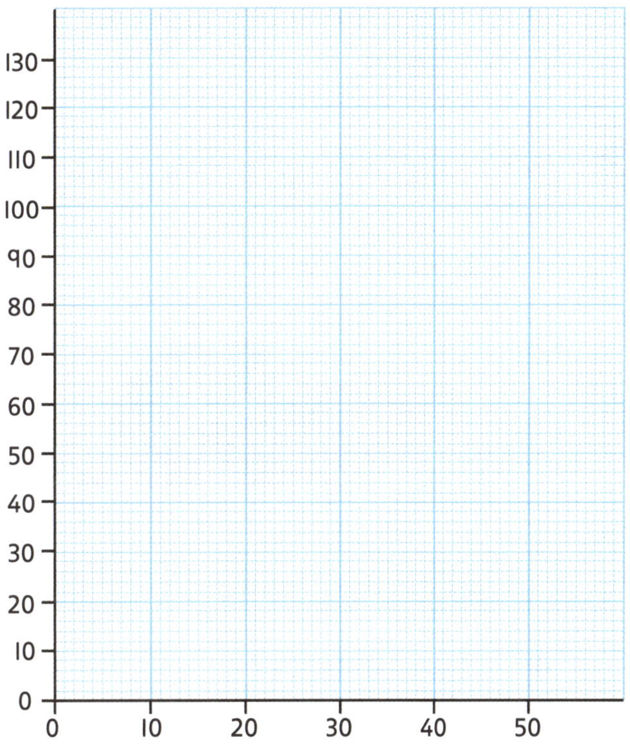

b) What should the learner do to be more confident that his results are reliable?

____

Choosing a method of separating mixtures

1 Complete the rules for choosing a method of separating.

- If one material is **magnetic**, use a ___________________________.

- If two solids have **grains of different sizes**, use a ___________________________.

- If there is a **solid in a liquid**, but the ___________________________ has **not dissolved**, use ___________________________.

- If there is a **solid dissolved in a liquid**, use ___________________________.

2 Write **one** method of separating each of these mixtures.

a) Iron and flour

____

b) Sand in water

____

c)   Sand and paperclips

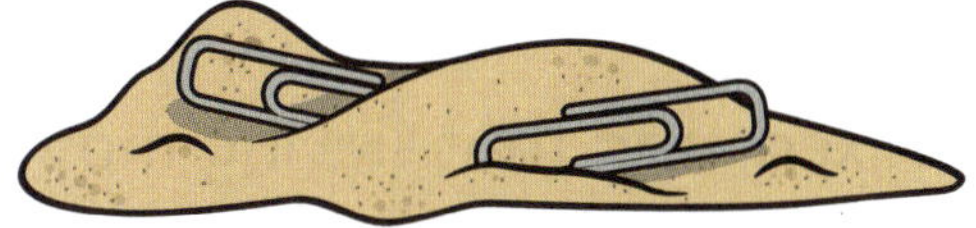

____

d)   Dry pasta and flour

____

e)   Sugar in water

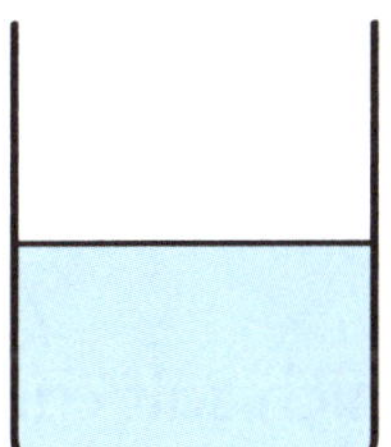

____

f)   Sand and gravel

____

What have I learned?

1 I understand that solids can be mixed, and that sieving may be used to separate some mixtures.

I know this because I can separate a mixture of

________________________ and ________________________ by sieving.

2 I can explain how filtration may be used to separate some solids from a liquid.

I know this because I can separate ________________________ and

________________________ by using filtration.

3 I understand that when a solid dissolves in water it forms a solution that **cannot** be separated by filtration.

I know this because I **cannot** separate ________________________

and ________________________ by using filtration.

4 I can describe ways in which simple substances such as sugar and salt can be dissolved more quickly.

I know this because I can write **three** ways in which salt can be dissolved faster.

1. ____

2. ____

3. ____

5 I can explain that when a solution is left with air around it the liquid will evaporate, leaving just the dissolved solid.

I know this because I can use this method to separate

_______________________ and _______________________.

6 I can use knowledge of solids, liquids and gases to decide how to separate mixtures. This includes sieving, using a magnet, filtering and evaporating.

I know this because I can write a mixture that can be separated by each of these methods.

Method	Example of mixture that can be separated using this method
sieving	
using a magnet	
filtering	
evaporating	

Earth and space

Earth and the Moon are part of our Solar System. The Sun is a star at the centre of our Solar System. Earth is just one of the planets in our Solar System orbiting the Sun. At night, we can see our Moon as it reflects light from the Sun.

In this topic we will learn:

- that the Sun is a star and is at the centre of our Solar System

- that Earth, the Sun and the Moon are part of the Solar System

- that planets are different sizes, and some have more than one moon

- how to describe the position and the movement of Earth, and other planets, relative to the Sun in our Solar System

- that ideas about the Solar System have changed and developed over time

- that Earth spins on its axis causing some parts of Earth to be in daylight when other parts are in darkness

- about Earth's rotation to explain the apparent movement of the Sun across the sky

- about how shadow length changes at different times of day.

Choose two key words from the box above.
Write or draw what they mean.

Our Solar System

1 a) Circle **one** term that describes the Sun.

a moon   a planet   a star   a system

b) Circle **one** term that describes Earth.

a moon   a planet   a star   a system

2 a) What do the words *solar* and *system* mean when we use them in the term Solar System?

solar: ____

____

system: ____

____

b) Tick (✓) **one** box in each table to name the object in the picture.

(i)

Earth	
the Moon	
the Solar System	
Saturn	
the Sun	

(ii)

Earth	
the Moon	
the Solar System	
Saturn	
the Sun	

(iii)

Earth	
the Moon	
the Solar System	
Saturn	
the Sun	

3 a) Circle the **largest** object in our Solar System.

Earth   the Moon

the International Space Station   the Sun

b) Which is the nearest star to Earth? _______________

4 a) (i) Describe the Sun using your textbook and some research of your own.

____

____

____

____

____

(ii) Why is it dangerous to look directly at the Sun?

____

b) Name **two** things that come to Earth from the Sun.

1. _________________________   2. _________________________

Earth, Sun and Moon

1 a) What are Earth, the Sun and the Moon all parts of?

____

b) How many moons does Earth have?

2 a) The picture shows Earth. Write what parts of Earth these areas show by their colour and texture.

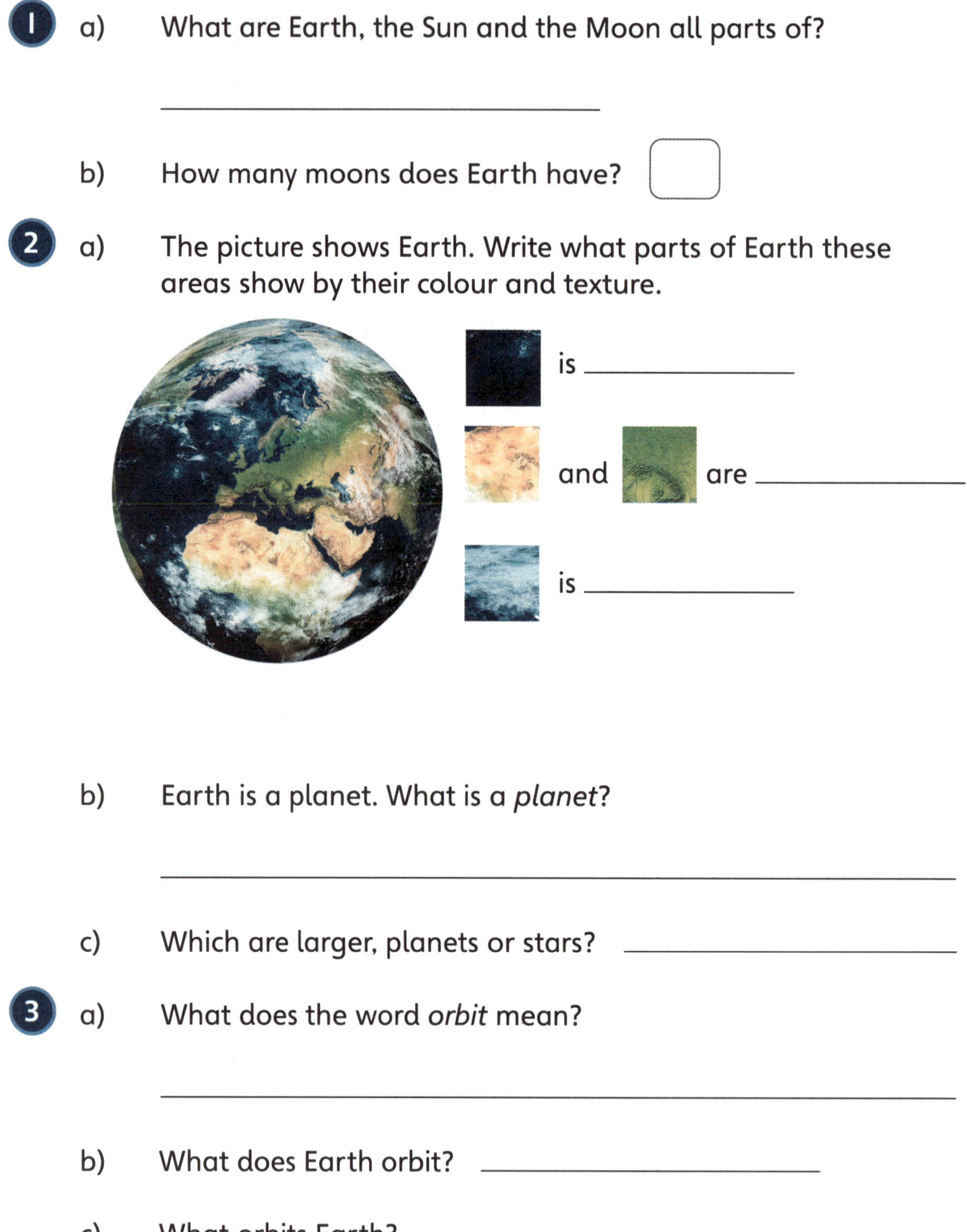

is _______________

and are _______________

is _______________

b) Earth is a planet. What is a *planet*?

____

c) Which are larger, planets or stars? _______________

3 a) What does the word *orbit* mean?

____

b) What does Earth orbit? _______________

c) What orbits Earth? _______________

4 The picture shows Earth, the Sun and the Moon.

a)   Write **Sun** on the correct part of the diagram.

b)   The Sun is a source of light. What does *source* mean?

____

c)   The Moon is **not** a source of light.

Explain why the Moon looks so bright from Earth.

____

____

5 Find out **three** facts about the Moon for yourself. Do not repeat things that you have already written about.

1. ____

____

2. ____

____

3. ____

____

Many moons

1 There are many moons in our Solar System.

The planets Mercury and Venus do not have any moons.

a) How many moons orbit Earth? _______________________

b) These models show four of the 79 moons of the planet Jupiter.

Name the **largest** of these four moons. _______________________

c) The picture shows the planet Mars. It has two moons.

(i) Draw a label, with a line and a word, to show which object is Mars.

(ii) Complete the sentences about Mars and its moons.

The larger moon is called _______________________.

The smaller moon is called _______________________.

Both moons orbit _______________________ while Mars

is orbiting the _______________________.

2 a) Use information from question 1 to complete this table.

Planet	Number of moons
Mercury	
Venus	
Earth	
Mars	
Jupiter	

b) Draw a bar chart to show this information.

Remember to put the names of planets without moons on the axis too.

Orbits and spins

1 a) Write the letter **O** for **orbit** or **S** for **spin** beside each of the **four** arrows on this diagram.

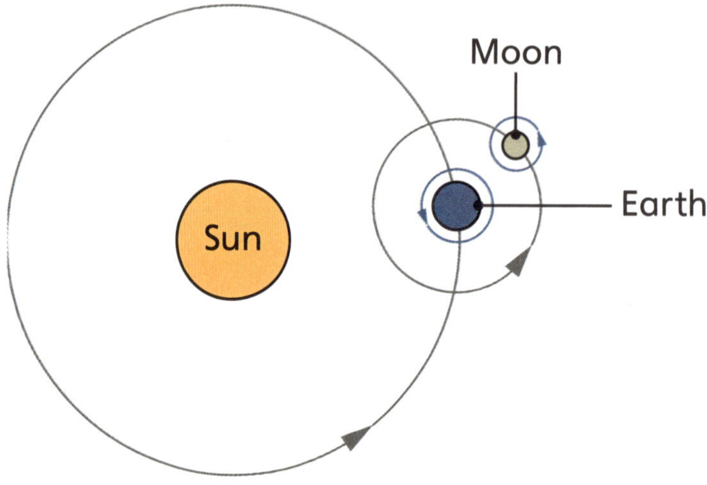

b) What do moons orbit? _______________________

c) This model shows how Earth spins.

    (i) What does the ball of string represent?

    ____

    (ii) What does the pin represent?

    ____

2 a) How long does it takes for Earth to orbit the Sun?

    ____

b) (i) How long does it take for Earth to rotate once?

    ____

    (ii) Write the time it takes in hours for Earth to rotate once.

    ________________________ hours

3 The table shows the time it takes for some planets to orbit the Sun once.

Planet	Number of whole Earth days it takes to orbit the Sun once
Mercury	88
Venus	225
Earth	365
Mars	687
Jupiter	4333

a) Which planet takes the **longest** time to orbit the Sun once?

____

b) Which planets orbit the Sun in shorter lengths of time than Earth?

____

c) The diagram shows the positions of these planets.

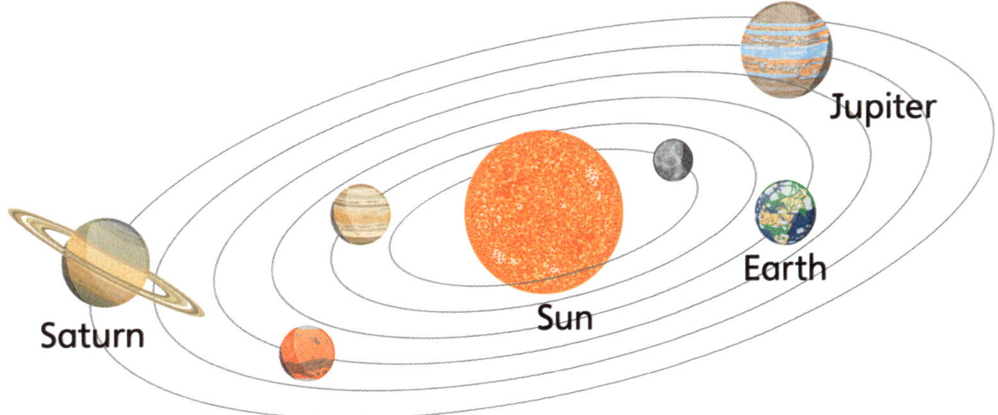

(i) Complete the sentence to show the pattern.

The further a planet is from the Sun, the _______________ time it takes to orbit once.

(ii) Predict how many days it takes for Saturn to orbit the Sun once.

The inner planets

1 a) How many planets are there in our Solar System? ☐

b) Name the **four** inner planets in order of distance from the Sun.

Sun _______________________   _______________________

_______________________   _______________________

c) Tick (✓) all the boxes that describe the inner planets.

rocky ☐

solid ☐

bigger than outer planets ☐

no rings ☐

2 The pictures in this question start with the planet closest to the Sun and then are in order of distance from the Sun.

a) Write the name of each planet above its picture.

b) (i) Write some facts about each planet.

(ii) Include **one** fact that is **not** in your textbook each time.

Name: _______________________

____

____

____

Fact not in textbook: _______________________

____

Name: _______________________

____

____

____

Fact not in textbook: _______________

____

Name: _______________________

____

____

____

Fact not in textbook: _______________

____

Name: _______________________

____

____

____

Fact not in textbook: _______________

____

The outer planets

1. The picture shows all eight planets in our Solar System.

Think of a sentence that helps you to remember their order.
Write it here.

____

____

2. The pictures in this question start with the outer planet that is closest to the Sun and then are in order of distance from the Sun.

a)   Name each planet above its picture.

b)   (i)   Write some facts about each planet.

   (ii)   Include **one** fact that is **not** in your textbook each time.

   Name: _______________________

   ____

   ____

   ____

   Fact not in textbook: _______________________________

   ____

Name: ______________________

____

____

____

____

Fact not in textbook: ______________________

____

Name: ______________________

____

____

____

____

Fact not in textbook: ______________________

____

Name: ______________________

____

____

____

____

Fact not in textbook: ______________________

____

Ideas about the Solar System

1 a) What is an *astronomer*?

____

b) Find the names of **four** different astronomers.

1. ____

2. ____

3. ____

4. ____

2 The diagram shows a very early model of the Solar System.

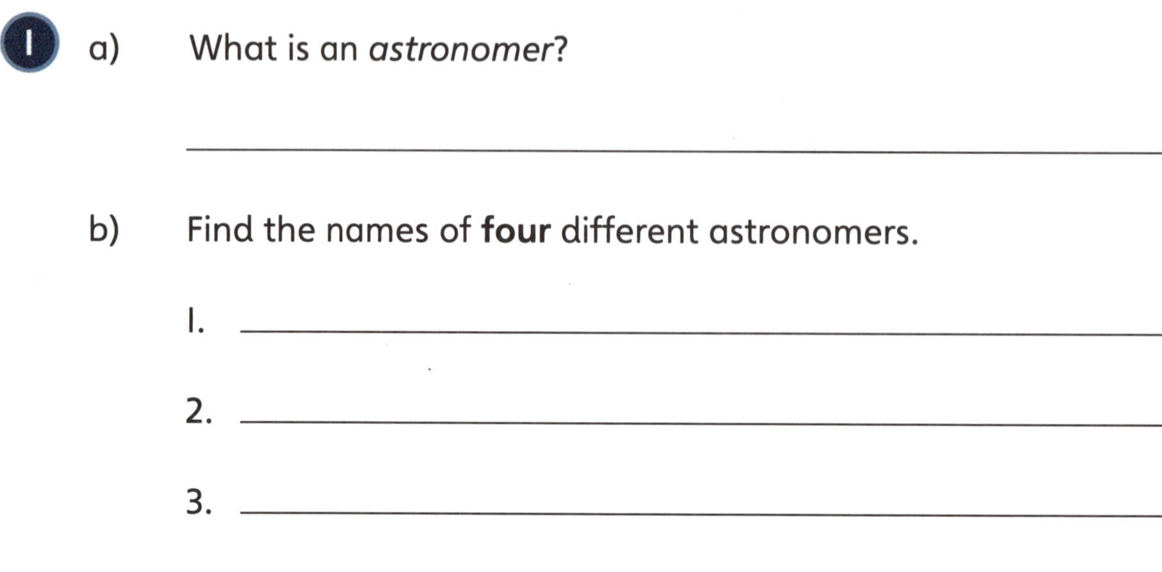

a) What is at the centre? _______________________

b) Describe what the Sun is doing.

____

c) Suggest why Uranus and Neptune are not shown on this model.

____

3. These drawings show two different models of our Solar System.

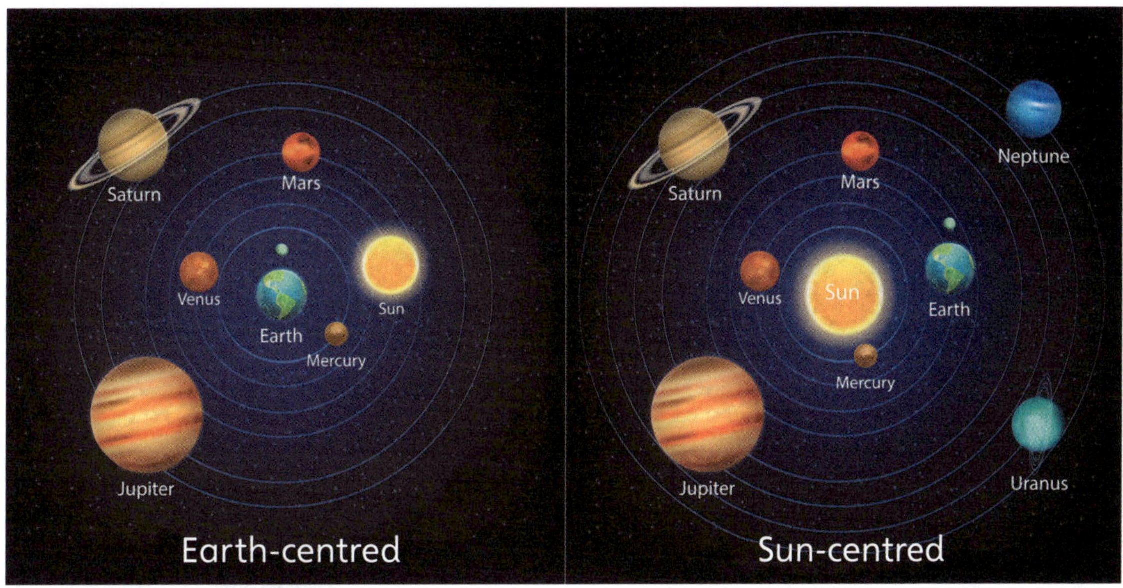

Model 1   **Model 2**

a)   Which model is more like the one that astronomers use today?

____

b)   Compare **Model 1** and **Model 2** to show **two** differences.

In Model 1 ____

but in Model 2 ____.

In Model 1 ____

but in Model 2 ____.

c)   Name **one** piece of equipment that helps astronomers to find out more about the Solar System.

____

____

Day and night

1 Write **day** or **night** under each picture.

_______________________   _______________________

_______________________   _______________________

2 The diagram shows Earth and the Sun.

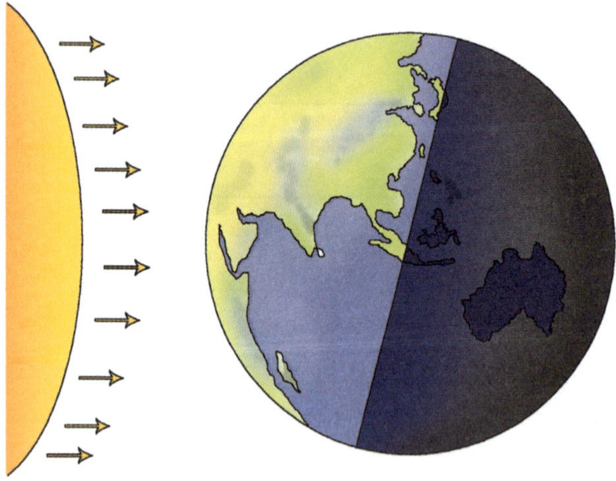

a) What do these arrows ⟶ represent? _______________________

b) Write **day** and **night** on the drawing of Earth.

c) Draw Earth's imaginary axis on the diagram.

3 a) (i)   How long does it take for Earth to spin once on its axis?

____

(ii) Now write this time using a different unit.

____

b) How many complete spins will Earth make in one year?

____

4 Mohsin makes a model of Earth and the Sun.

He sticks a paper butterfly   onto the model Earth.

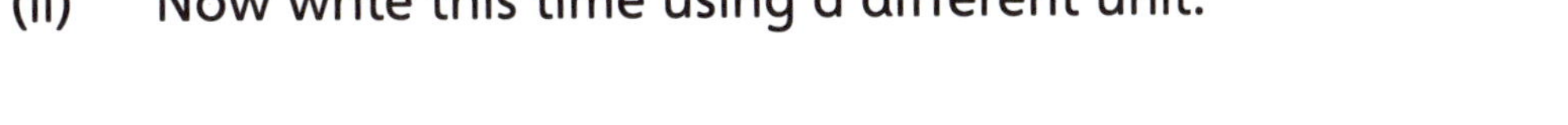

a) Is it day or night for the butterfly? ___________________________

b) Mohsin turns the model Earth to show where it has spun to after 12 hours.

(i) Draw where the butterfly is now.

(ii) Is it day or night for the butterfly now? ___________________

Shadow patterns

1 a) Label **light** and **dark** on this picture using a line and the word each time.

b) Complete the sentences.

We need light to ________________________ things.

Darkness is the absence of ________________________.

2 a) Write these words under the correct part of this drawing.

| shadow | light source | opaque object | wall |

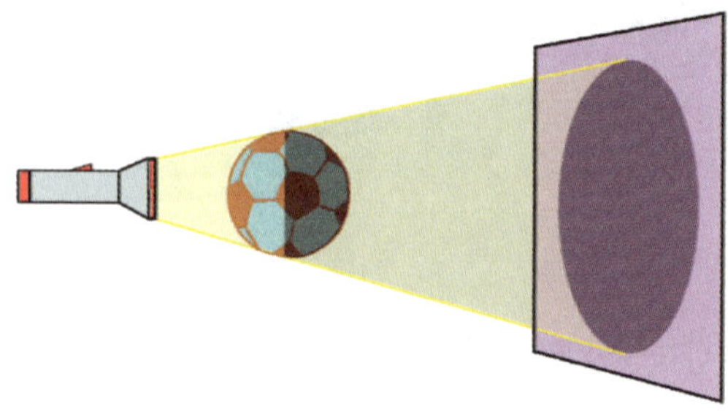

b) Explain how the round shadow is formed.

____

____

3 Do the investigation on page 123 of your textbook with a partner.

a) Write your scientific question.

____

b)   (i)   What are you changing?

____

     (ii) What are you measuring?

____

c)   Record your results in this table.

Other observations include the relative position of the Sun at that time of day.

Time	Length of shadow in cm	Other observations

d)   Do your results show a pattern? Describe the pattern.

____

____

e)   Your partner started with their back to the Sun and stood in the same position each time.

What did you observe about the Sun's relative position each time?

____

____

Why do shadows change?

1 a)   Name the light source in **Picture 1**. ______________________

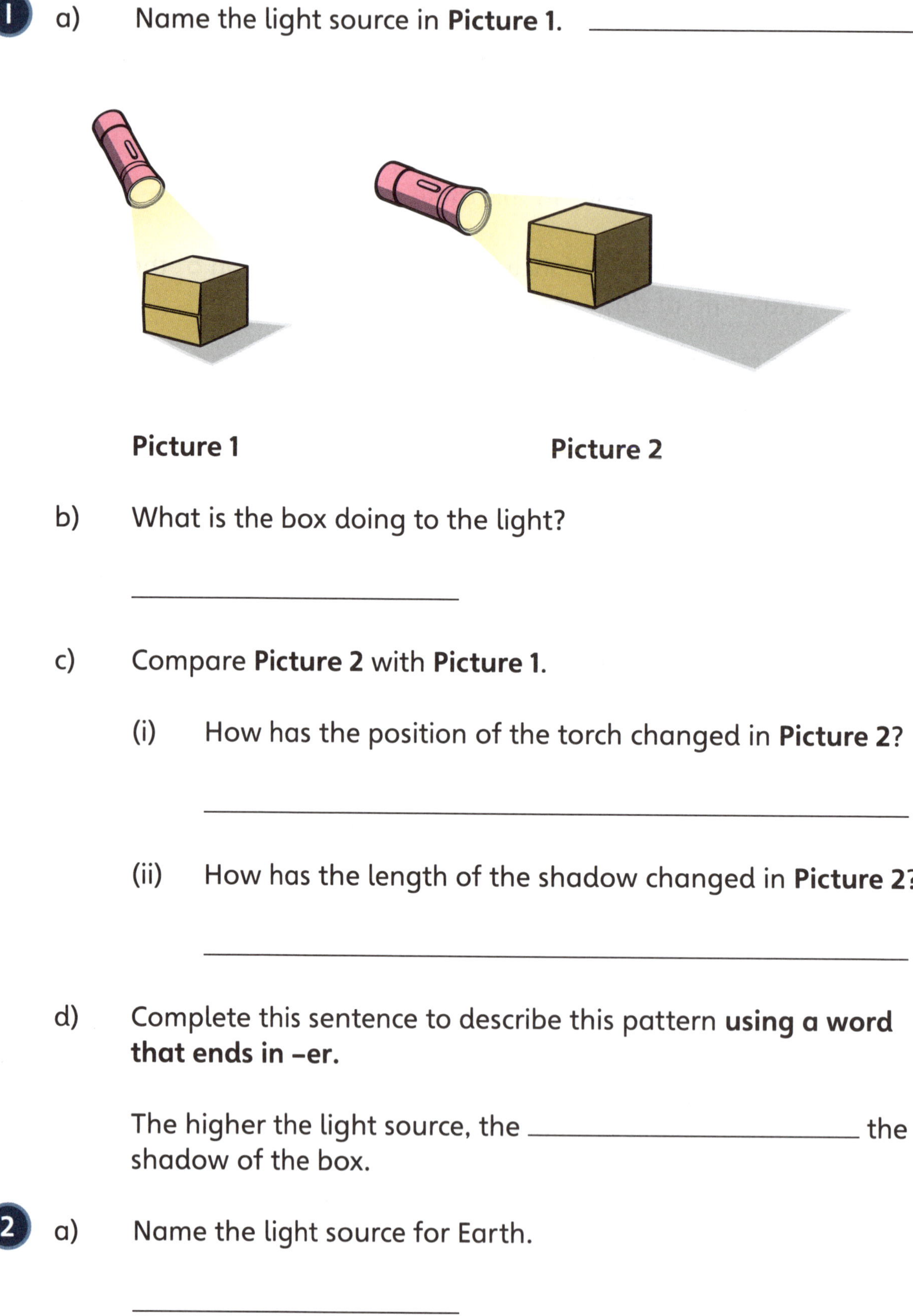

Picture 1   **Picture 2**

b)   What is the box doing to the light?

____

c)   Compare **Picture 2** with **Picture 1**.

(i)   How has the position of the torch changed in **Picture 2**?

____

(ii)   How has the length of the shadow changed in **Picture 2**?

____

d)   Complete this sentence to describe this pattern **using a word that ends in –er.**

The higher the light source, the ____________________ the shadow of the box.

2 a)   Name the light source for Earth.

____

b)   Complete the pictures below so that each one shows **the Sun and a shadow** of the tree.

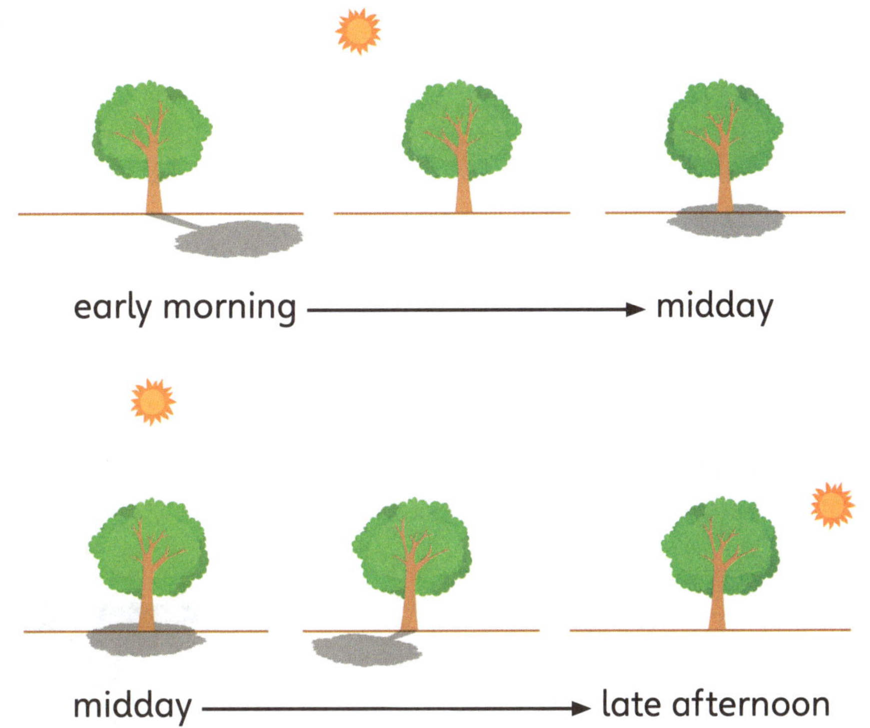

c)   The Sun is **not** moving. Explain why the Sun is in different positions in the pictures.

____

____

d)   Read question 1 d) again, then complete these sentences.

The higher we see the Sun in the sky, the

________________________ the shadow of the tree.

The ________________________ we see the Sun in the sky, the

________________________ the shadow of the tree.

Sundials

1. This learner is walking to school in the morning.

    How do these things show it is morning?

    a) The length of his shadow

    ____

    b) The position of the Sun

    ____

2. a) What is a sundial used for?

    ____

    ____

    b) Label the **shadow** of the metal bar on the picture.

3. A child makes this sundial on a beach. Four possible positions that the Sun could be in have been drawn.

a)   Circle the **one** Sun you think is most likely to be making this shadow.

b)   Suggest **one** improvement the child could make to this sundial.

____

4 Make your own sundial.

a)   Draw it or stick in a photograph of it.

b)   Describe how you used it.

____

____

c)   Write **one** way you could improve what you did.

____

____

____

1 I understand that the Sun is a star and is at the centre of our Solar System. I also understand that Earth, the Sun and the Moon are part of the Solar System, and that Earth is a planet with one moon.

I know this because I can label Sun, Earth and Moon on this drawing.

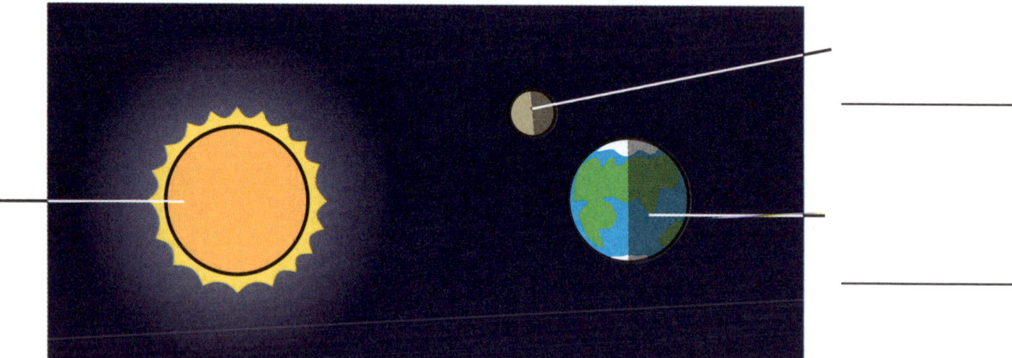

2 I understand that planets are different sizes, and some have more than one moon.

I can describe the position and the movement of Earth and other planets relative to the Sun in our Solar System.

I know this because I can name **two** planets with more moons than Earth.

1. ____

2. ____

I also know this because I can name these planets.

3 I can describe the movement of the Moon relative to Earth, and Earth and the other planets relative to the Sun, using the term *orbit*.

I understand that ideas about the Solar System have changed and developed over time.

I know this because I can complete these sentences.

The Moon _______________________ Earth.

Earth and the other planets orbit the _______________________.

Many years ago, astronomers thought that _______________________ was at the centre of the Solar System, not the Sun.

4 I can explain that Earth spins on its axis causing some parts of Earth to be in daylight when other parts are in darkness.

I know this because I can label **day** and **night** on this model.

5 I can use the idea of Earth's rotation to explain the apparent movement of the Sun across the sky. I understand how shadow length changes at different times of day.

I know this because I can draw the missing **shadow** and the missing **Sun** on these diagrams.

Seeing and reflecting

Light from a light source appears to travel in straight lines. We see things because this light travels to our eyes. Objects around us reflect light, which then travels to our eyes. Light reflects off shiny surfaces. We use smooth, shiny surfaces to look at our reflection.

In this topic we will learn:

- that light comes from a source and appears to travel in straight lines

- that we see things because light travels from light sources to our eyes or from light sources to objects and then to our eyes

- that light can be reflected from shiny surfaces and, when reflected, the light changes direction

- that smooth and shiny surfaces reflect light well, but light is more scattered when it is reflected from a dull surface

- to recognise and give simple explanations for differences between shadows and reflections.

Choose two key words from the box above.
Write or draw what they mean.

Light in straight lines

1 a)   Name these sources of light.

b)   Which sense organ do we use to see things? ______________

c)   (i)   Complete the sentence to explain how this person can see the light.

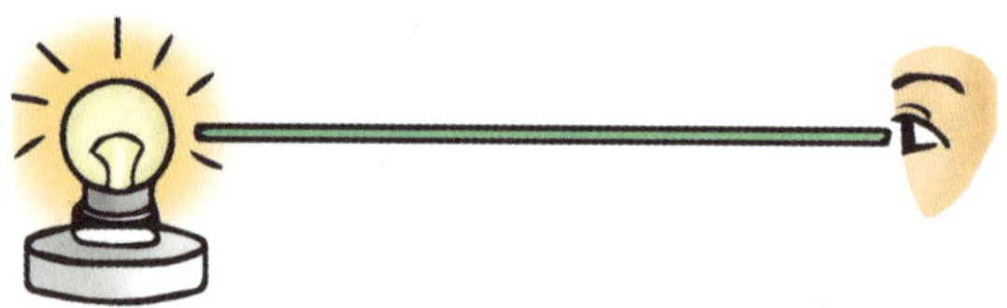

Light travels from a light ________________________ to

the person's ________________________.

    (ii)   Complete the sentence to explain why this person **cannot** see the light.

Light travels in ________________________ lines.

It cannot ________________________ around corners.

2 A learner has three cards, each with a hole in the centre.

The cards are held upright using sticky tack. There is a book behind them.

a)　The learner shines the torch on the first card.

(i)　Predict what he sees on the book.

____

(ii)　Explain why you think this.

____

____

b)　Try doing this investigation yourself, if you can.

What happens? Was your prediction correct?

____

____

3 Another learner uses this equipment.

Use your knowledge of how light travels to explain why the round shadow forms.

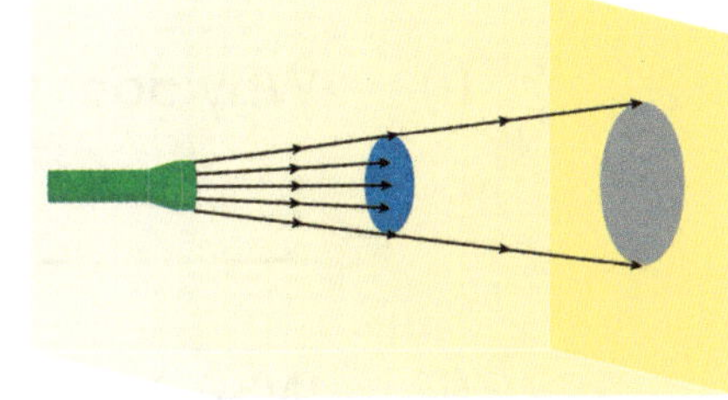

____

____

____

Shiny surfaces

1 a) Circle all the **sources** of light.

b) Write **one** word to describe the objects you did **not** circle.

____

c) In the dark, the Moon and the water are both bright.

(i) Why does the Moon look bright?

____

(ii) Why does the water look bright?

____

____

2 Complete the sentence about light.

When an object reflects light, the light still travels in straight

__________________________, but it changes __________________________.

3 a)   Complete the ray diagram to show the ray of light from the bulb reflecting off the shiny surface. Use a ruler.

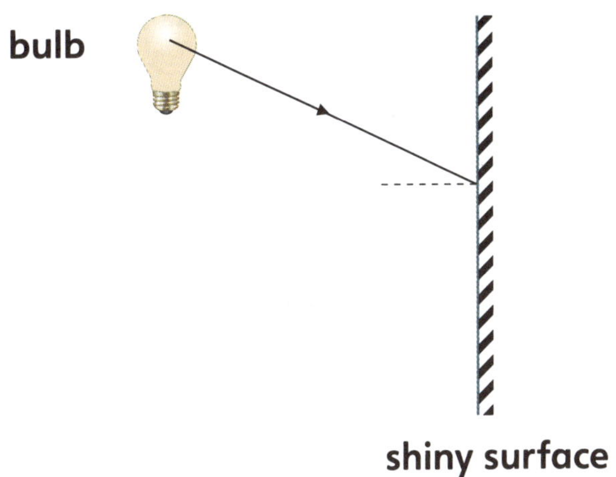

b)   Why must you use a ruler for ray diagrams?

____

4 Draw a ray of light from the torch reflecting off this mirror. Use a ruler.

Reflecting light

1 Name some objects in your classroom, home or outside that are **shiny** and some that are **dull**.

Some objects may have a dull part and a shiny part. Think about where you will write the names of those.

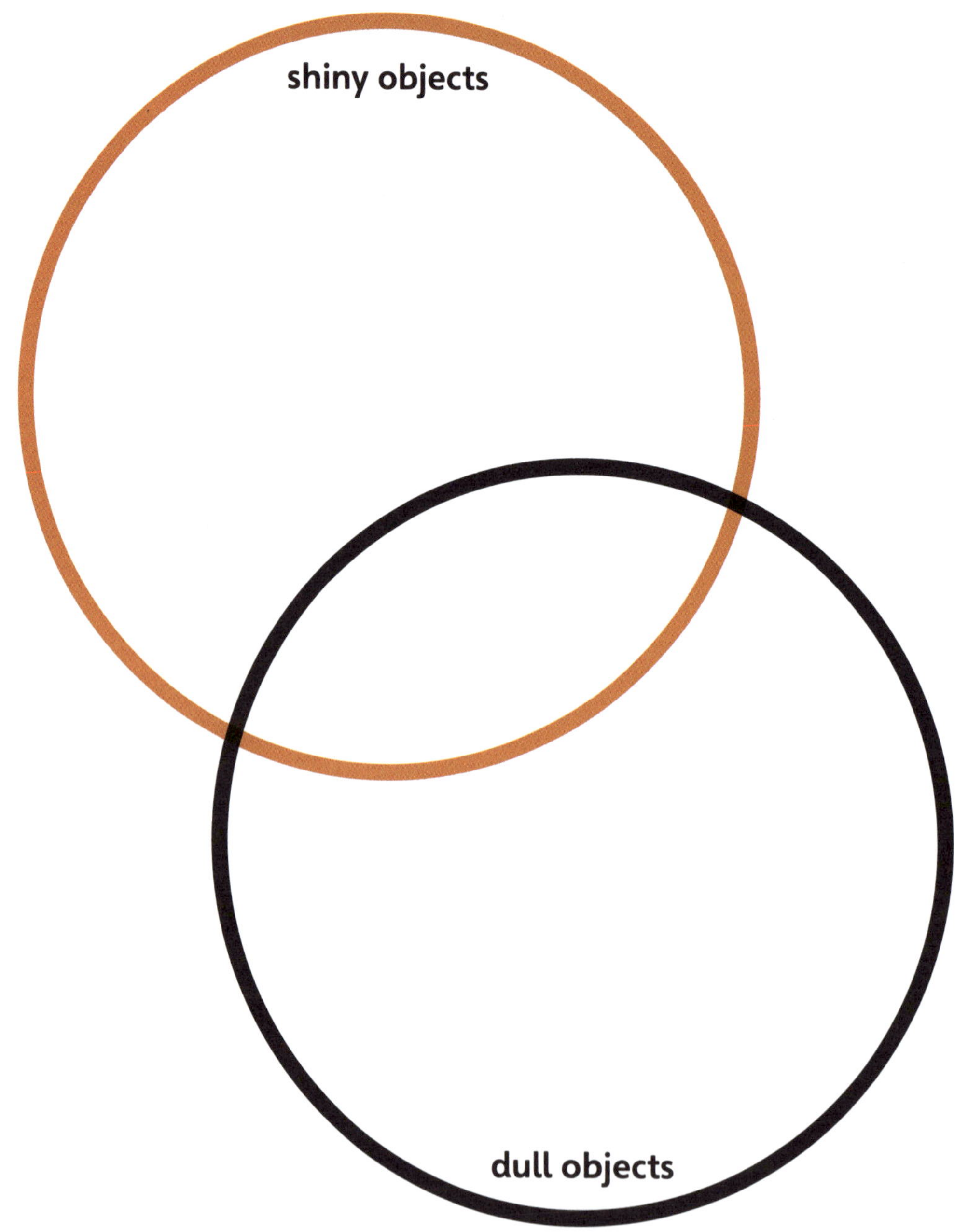

2 a) Complete the sentences about shiny and dull surfaces.

b) Draw the reflected rays from the shiny and the dull surfaces. Use a ruler.

Shiny surfaces reflect all the rays of _______________________

from a source at the same _______________________.

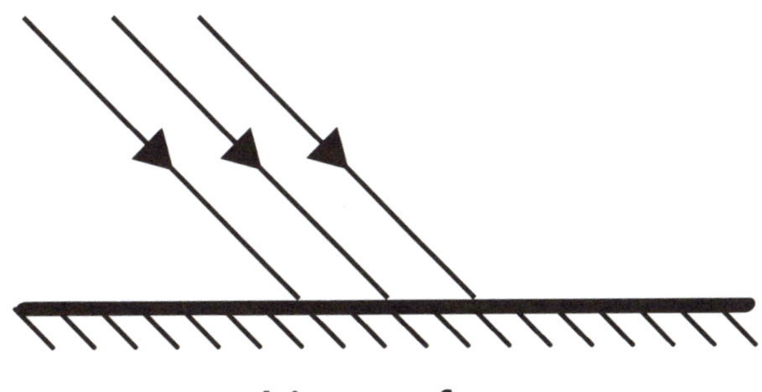

shiny surface

Dull surfaces do not reflect _______________________ well.

Any light that is reflected from them is _______________________ in many directions.

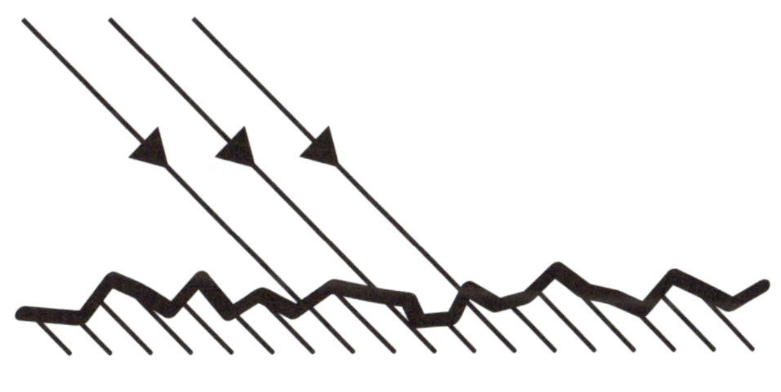

dull surface

How do we see objects?

1 Complete the sentences using only the words from the box. You can use each word more than once.

> eyes   source   object

We see things because light travels from a light ____________________

to our ____________________.

We also see things when light travels from a light

____________________ to an ____________________.

Light that reflects from the ____________________ travels to our

____________________.

2 a) Draw an arrow on the ray of light to show its direction.

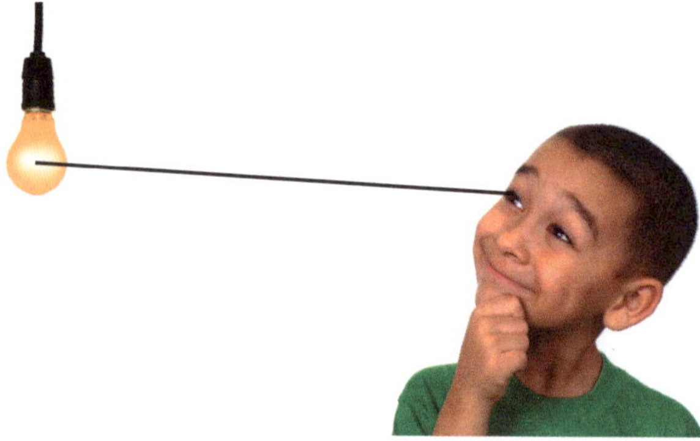

b) Draw a ray of light to show how the person sees the television show. Use a ruler.

3 Complete the ray diagram to show how the learner sees the words in the book. Use a ruler.

4 Draw a ray diagram to show how the boy sees the spider. Use a ruler. Remember to show the direction the light travels in.

Shadow or reflection?

1 a) (i) Label the **shadow**.

(ii) What is the opaque object? _______________________

b) Explain how this shadow is made.

____

____

____

c) Tick (✓) **all** the statements about shadows that are correct.

A shadow is always the same **shape** as the opaque object. ☐

Light bends around an opaque object to make a shadow. ☐

A shadow is always the same **size** as the opaque object. ☐

Light rays do not travel through opaque objects. ☐

A shadow is always **larger** than the opaque object. ☐

2 a) Circle **two** words to describe surfaces that reflect light well.

black   dull   shiny   smooth   rough

b) Name some objects that reflect light well and some that do not.

Objects that ...	
... reflect light well	... do not reflect light well

c) This surface reflects light well.

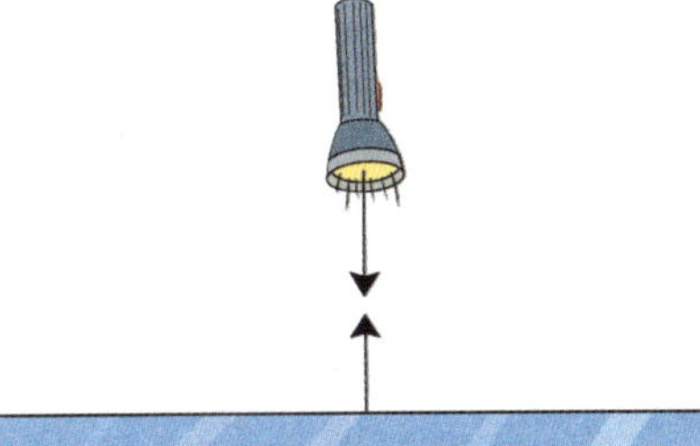

Describe what happens to the ray of light from the torch when it hits the surface.

____

d) This surface also reflects light well.

Draw the reflected ray with a ruler and show its direction.

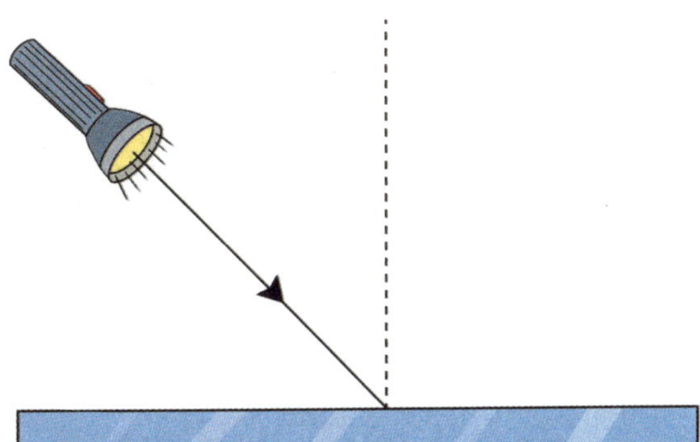

Investigating safety clothing

1   a)   Write about a place where you have seen people wearing safety clothing.

What job were they doing?

____

____

b)   This safety clothing is made of two different materials, **A** and **B**. Materials **A** and **B** have different functions.

Describe what each material does.

A   _______________________________________

B   _______________________________________

2   Traffic cones are used to stop people driving on part of a road that is closed.

They work well in the day and at night.

a)   What makes the traffic cone easy to see in the **day**?

traffic cone

____

b)   (i)   Name **two** light sources on a road at **night**.

1. _________________   2. _________________

(ii)   What makes the traffic cone easy to see at **night**?

____

3 Plan an investigation to find out which safety clothing is best to wear at night.

a) Write your scientific question.

____

b) (i) What will you change? _______________________

(ii) How will you decide which safety clothing is best?

____

____

c) What will you use as a light source? _______________________

d) Write **two** things that you will keep the same.

1. ____

2. ____

e) Draw the results table you need for your investigation.

f) Write a conclusion that answers your scientific question.

____

____

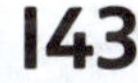

What have I learned?

1 I understand that light comes from a source and appears to travel in straight lines.

I know this because I can label the light source in this picture and explain why the learner cannot see it.

____

____

2 I can explain that we see things because light travels from light sources to our eyes or from light sources to objects and then to our eyes.

I can use the idea that light appears to travel in straight lines to explain that objects are seen because they give out or reflect light into our eyes.

I know this because I can draw a ray of light to show how light from the bulb allows the boy to see the cake.

3 I understand that light can be reflected from shiny surfaces and, when reflected, the light changes direction.

I know this because I can complete this ray diagram showing how a ray of light is reflected from this shiny surface.

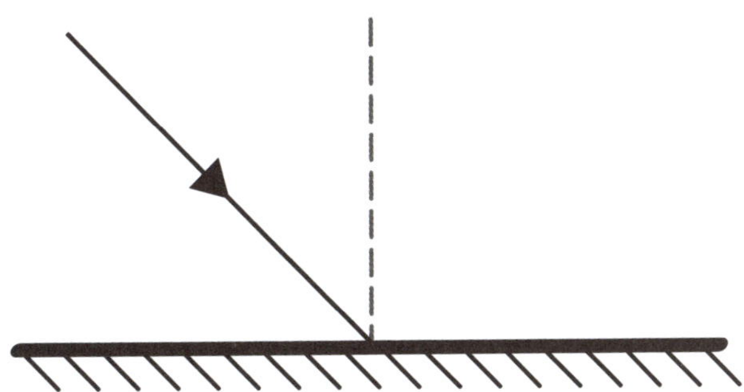

4 I understand that smooth and shiny surfaces reflect light well, but light is more scattered when it is reflected from a dull surface.

I know this because I can show my teacher where I completed ray diagrams showing this on page 137 of this workbook.

5 I can recognise and give simple explanations for differences between shadows and reflections.

I know this because I can complete these sentences.

A shadow is formed when an ________________________ object

________________________ light.

A reflection happens when light rays hit a shiny object and change

________________________.

My notes

My notes

My notes

My notes

(key: b-bottom; c-centre; l-left; r-right; t-top)

Non-Prominent Image Credit(s):

123RF GB LIMITED: Anton Starikov 86t, Cathy Frost 126b, Chad Zuber 65, Christos Georghiou 116t, Dmitry Rukhlenko 134 L-R 3c, elyrae 82 T-B 2, lobster20 17c, magone 56 R T-B 2, Olga Yastremska 59 L-R 1t, Siarhei Holub 56 L T-B 2, udaix.com 140t, viktoriya chursina 56 L T-B 1; **Alamy Images:** Gina Kelly 12b, Panther Media GmbH 35, Corbin17 46 L-R 1c, Science History Images 46 L-R 2c, Nerthuz 115t; **PEARSON EDUCATION LIMITED:** Arvind Singh Negi/Red Reef Design Studio L-R 1b, 120 L-R 2b, 132b, 132c, 134 L-R 2t, 13t, 144, 145, Cheuk-king Lo 15, Coleman Yuen 83 L-R 4t, 92b, HL Studios 49, Joey Chan 100b, 90c, Mark Turner. Beehive Illustration 44c, Mohammed Ali 10c, 122c, 71, 86 L-R 2c, 87t, 89t, Mohd Suhail 109, Oxford Designers & Illustrators Ltd 135t, 45b, 45c, 45t, 57, 69b, 91, PDQ Digital Media Solutions Ltd 10t, 111, 138b, 139t, 14, 55, Trevor Clifford 93, Utsav Academy and Art Studio 11c; **SCIENCE PHOTO LIBRARY LIMITED:** GIPHOTOSTOCK 86c, MARTYN F. CHILLMAID 90b; **SHUTTERSTOCK:** 19 STUDIO 114b, 115c, 116b, 117b, 117t, 3445128471 138 L-R 2c, 139b, 58 L-R 2b, A Kisel 34t, aekikuis 125c, 125t, 129b, Afonkin_Y 101 T-B 2, AKIllustration 68t, 77 T-B 1, Alex Staroseltsev 106 T-B 1b, AlexLMX 128b, allex wijaya 23 L-R 2b, Alones 115b, Amanda Carden 106 T-B 2b, 132 L-R 3t, Anastasia Boiko 120 L-R 1t, 120 L-R 2t, Andrea Izzotti 28c, andreev-studio.ru 46t, Anke van Wyk 9t, Anna Nikonorova 32t, ArtAdisorn 120 L-R 1c, Artur Synenko 132 L-R 1t, asawinimages 16c, AVN Photo Lab 12t, bazilpp 90t, bigacis 58t, Billion Photos 56 R T-B 1, BlueRingMedia 73 T-B 3, 77 T-B 2, blue-sea.cz 39c, Bruno Rodrigues B Silva 82 T-B 5, Bukhavets Mikhail 30t, ChockdeePermploysiri 107t, DImin 113b, Dariush M 13 L-R 1c, 13 L-R 2c, DenisMArt 82 T-B 1, Denny Davidson 118c, Diana Taliun 83 L-R 6t, Diego Barucco 110t, dugdax 6b, Elenall 110c, Elnur 142t, Emilio100 82 T-B 3, enrouteksm 6 T-B 1c, Eric Isselee 70t, Eric Valenne geostory 39t, Evgeniya Uvarova 56 R T-B 3, fotohunter 59 L-R 2t, Four Oaks 40b, FrameAngel 132 L-R 2t, Fulcanelli 38b, Gabriela Trojanowska 58 L-R 3b, GraphicsRF.com 8b, 9b, grayjay 100c, grayjay 101 T-B 4, guentermanaus 26c, helena0105 134 L-R 2c, homydesign 85b, Ingrid Prats 134b, James Marvin Phelps 31 L-R 1c, Jan Kaliciak 86 L-R 1c, JCLobo 134 L-R 1c, Jiri Hera 58 L-R 4b, JKIWA 133b, Joaquin Corbalan P 43c, jokerpro 134 L-R 3t, koosen 83 L-R 2t, koya979 142b, KYTan 83 L-R 3t, Lifestyle Travel Photo 132 L-R 4t, 138 L-R 1c, 139 L-R 1c, Lightspring 73 T-B 1, 77 T-B 3, M.Stasy 121b, 121c, Maarten Zeehandelaar 32b, Macrovector 69 L-R 1t, 69 L-R 2t, 69 L-R 3t, 69 L-R 4t, Madlen 85c, Marek Tr 101 T-B 3, marilyn barbone 64 T-B 1b, Mas Akhi 64 T-B 2b, max dallocco 108c, Max Topchii 23 L-R 1b, Max_555 17t, mbarredo 6 T-B 2c, methal819 42 L-R 2c, MidoSemsem 56 R T-B 4, Mishna 38c, MK Lasek 33t, MNStudio 44t, Modvector 82 T-B 4, My-Sun-Shine 121c, NASA images 117c, Natalia van D 42b, New Africa 92t, newelle 139 L-R 2c, Niraelanor 16 T-B 2b, Nungning20 84c, Olha1981/Shuterstock 37 L-R 1t, 37 L-R 2t, 37 L-R 3t, 37 L-R 4t, Olya Maximenko 16 T-B 1b, photka 83 L-R 1t, pjmorley 56 L T-B 3, PRILL 88c, PS Media House 31 L-R 2c, redknapper 83t, Reidl 56 L T-B 4, renklerin kafasi 135b, 141b, 141c, rktz 83c, 84t, Roelof87 40c, Roger de Montfort 17b, Ropsie Chids 87c, Rudmer Zwerver 33c, S. Mahanantakul 15b, sarin nana 15c, SciePro 73 T-B 2, SciePro 77 T-B 4, Selyutina Olga 134 L-R 1t, Sergey Dzyuba 32c, Shuttertum 88t, 89b, Siberian Art 119t, silvae 122t, steveball 126c, Studio Barcelona 126b, Sytilin Pavel 42t, Tanya_mtv 58 L-R 2c, Tarcisio Schnaider 26t, TheBlackRhino 10b, think4photop 11t, Tim UR 58 L-R 1b, trabantos 31t, Vaclav Sebek 8c, Vectorfair 120 L-R 2c, View Apart 28t, Viktar Malyshchyts 58 L-R 5b, WindOfHope 8t, xpixel 101 T-B 1, yavuzunlu 83 L-R 5t, Yeti studio 58 L-R 1c, Yuliia Liesova 121b, 121c, YuRi Photolife 42 L-R 1c, Zebra-Studio 12c, Zeng Wei Jun 33b,

Non-Prominent Text Credit(s):

CHINA STATE FORESTRY ADMINISTRATION PANDA CENSUS: 34, ROYAL OSTEOPOROSIS SOCIETY: 61.

All other images © Pearson Education